# YAHWEH
# Is **NOT** the
# LORD
## JEHOVAH

יְהֹוָה

## The Devilish Deception
## of the
## Hebrew Roots Movement

## Edward Hendrie

Behold, God is my salvation; I will trust, and not be afraid: for the LORD JEHOVAH is my strength and my song; he also is become my salvation. (Isaiah 12:2)

GREAT MOUNTAIN PUBLISHING

Other books from Great Mountain Publishing®
● 9/11-Enemies Foreign and Domestic
● Solving the Mystery of BABYLON THE GREAT
● The Anti-Gospel
● Bloody Zion
● What Shall I Do to Inherit Eternal Life?
● Murder, Rape, and Torture in a Catholic Nunnery
● Antichrist: The Beast Revealed
● The Greatest Lie on Earth
● The Greatest Lie on Earth (Expanded Edition)
● Rome's Responsibility for the Assassination of Abraham Lincoln
● The Damnable Heresy of Salvation by Dead Faith (Expanded Edition)
● The Sphere of Influence
● Vaccine Danger: Quackery and Sin
● Hoax of Biblical Proportions

Available at:
https://greatmountainpublishing.com
https://play.google.com
www.barnesandnoble.com
www.amazon.com

Edward Hendrie rests on the authority of the Holy Bible alone for doctrine. He considers the Holy Bible to be the inspired and inerrant word of God. Favorable citation by Edward Hendrie to an authority outside the Holy Bible on a particular issue should not be interpreted to mean that he agrees with all of the doctrines and beliefs of the cited authority. All Scripture references are to the Authorized (King James) Version of the Holy Bible, unless otherwise indicated.

# Table of Contents

# Introduction

This book is excerpted from *Hoax of Biblical Proportions*, with some additional material. That book reveals how God's inspired King James Holy Bible exposes Satan's profane Bibles.

Satan knows that God has promised to preserve his words found in the Holy Scriptures, so it would be futile for him to try to destroy them. Thus, Satan's strategy is to obscure God's words by flooding the world with counterfeit Bibles. That way, he can flimflam people into reading his corrupt Bibles instead of God's infallible Scriptures. The devil can then lead men astray from the true gospel.

ISBN: 978-1-943056-18-7

*Hoax of Biblical Proportions* proves that the Authorized (King James) Version of the Holy Bible is given by inspiration of God. It reveals how Satan is using profane Bible versions to divert the world away from God's inspired Holy Scriptures. The changes in the new Bible

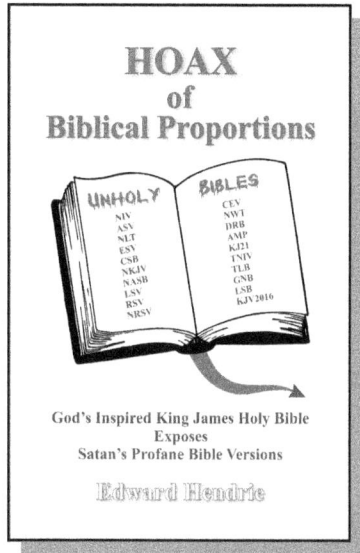

1

versions are not merely cosmetic for ease of reading, as claimed by the publishers; they change doctrine. The new Bible versions confuse churches and demoralize the world by proclaiming a different Jesus and a different gospel from what is in God's inspired King James Holy Bible.

Part and parcel of the deception in the new Bible versions is changing the name of God from Jehovah to Yahweh. That change has been popularized by the Hebrew Roots (a.k.a. Sacred Name) movement. Jehovah is the proper English translation of the Hebrew Tetragrammaton (יהוה) (YHVH). The Hebrew Roots movement invokes Yahweh in place of Jehovah. They falsely claim that Yahweh is the proper pronunciation of the Tetragrammaton. In actuality, invoking Yahweh is a trick to get people to worship a devil in place of God Almighty, Jehovah. God's name is Jehovah; Yahweh is a heathen storm god.

I excerpted the information from *Hoax of Biblical Proportions* to have a single publication dedicated to helping people understand the devilish deception of the Hebrew Roots movement in its effort to replace the worship of Almighty God, Jehovah, with a heathen god, Yahweh.

# 1 Jehovah (Not Yahweh) Is LORD

**M**any have probably heard people claiming to be "Christians" call God "Yahweh." Many are a little surprised, having never before heard that name for God. The persons using the word take great pride in displaying their understanding of the "true" name of God. The speaker and listener usually don't know that Yahweh is NOT the proper name for God. In reality, Yahweh is the name for a heathen weather god.

God's true name is **Jehovah**. We find in Exodus 6:2-3, that God reveals his proper name, **Jehovah**.

> And God spake unto Moses, and said unto him, I am the Lord: And I appeared unto Abraham, unto Isaac, and unto Jacob, by the name of God Almighty, but by my name **JEHOVAH** was I not known to them. Exodus 6:2-3 (AV)

Jehovah is the proper English translation of the Hebrew Tetragrammaton (י ה ו ה) (YHVH). The minions of Satan in the Hebrew Roots (a.k.a. Sacred Name) movement have hoodwinked their followers into using the name Yahweh in place of Jehovah. They ignorantly think that Yahweh is the correct pronunciation of the Hebrew Tetragrammaton (י ה ו ה) (YHVH), rather than

Jehovah. They are wrong. Yahweh is a satanic trap set for the unlearned and gullible. It subverts people into worshiping a devil, Yahweh, in place of God Almighty, Jehovah. God's name is Jehovah; Yahweh is a heathen tribal god.

Dr. James White, who promotes the corrupt new Bible versions, says Jehovah is a false pronunciation of the Tetragrammaton: "Now, 'Jehovah' is a false pronunciation of the Hebrew word 'YHWH,' correctly pronounced 'Yahweh.' This is God's 'personal' name in the Old Testament."[1] This corruption is finding its way into the modern Bible translations. For example, the New Living Translation (NLT) has changed the passage where God identifies himself as Jehovah to having God identify himself as Yahweh.

| AV | NLT |
|---|---|
| And God spake unto Moses, and said unto him, I am **the LORD**: And I appeared unto Abraham, unto Isaac, and unto Jacob, by the name of God Almighty, but by my name **JEHOVAH** was I not known to them. Exodus 6:2-3 (AV) | And God said to Moses, "I am **Yahweh**—'the Lord.' I appeared to Abraham, to Isaac, and to Jacob as E l - S h a d d a i — ' G o d Almighty'—but I did not reveal my name, **Yahweh**, to them. Exodus 6:2-3 (NLT) |

James White promotes the Legacy Standard Bible (LSB) as being more accurate than the King James Bible.[2] The LSB replaces God's name, Jehovah, with the name Yahweh. Using the name Yahweh is not a different way of pronouncing God's name. It is a replacement of God. Indeed, James White is emphatic that God's name is NOT Jehovah. He claims that God's true name is Yahweh, and it is impossible for his name to be Jehovah. "Yahweh is unquestionably the best pronunciation of the Divine name. **Jehovah is not even possible.**"[3] James White and the LSB have rejected the true God, Jehovah, and replaced him with a heathen tribal god, Yahweh.

| AV | LSB |
|---|---|
| And God spake unto Moses, and said unto him, I am **the LORD**: And I appeared unto Abraham, unto Isaac, and unto Jacob, by the name of God Almighty, but by my name **JEHOVAH** was I not known to them. (Exodus 6:2-3 AV) | God spoke further to Moses and said to him, "I am **Yahweh**; and I appeared to Abraham, Isaac, and Jacob, as God Almighty, but by My name, **Yahweh**, I was not known to them." (Exodus 6:2-3 LSB) |

John MacArthur, a world-famous preacher and President of the Master's University and Seminary, announced the publication of the Legacy Standard Bible (LSB) by making particular note of the use of Yahweh in place of Jehovah. MacArthur states that it is of utmost importance that Christians know God's name. He states that calling God Yahweh is one of the principal reasons he considers the LSB "a priceless treasure—an amazing effort." But he obfuscates what he has actually done. He claims he is more reverent to God by stating his name, which he thinks is Yahweh, instead of the LORD. But he does not reveal that he is changing the name of the eternal God from Jehovah to Yahweh. To understand that, you would have to read Exodus 6:3, Psalms 83:18, Isaiah 12:2, and Isaiah 26:4 in the LSB.

> For about a year, linguistic scholars of the Master's University and the Master's Seminary have been working on a translation called the Legacy Standard Bible. It's come to completion. Now, the first printed form of it is the New Testament Psalms and Proverbs. It's the best English translation I have ever read. It's the most diligently prepared translation. **And one of the wonderful**

5

features of it is it calls God by the name he asked to be remembered by. When you say LORD, you're talking about his sovereignty. In all English Bibles, Yahweh is translated LORD in upper case letters. But that just repeats Adonai. It doesn't give you the name of God, which is the covenant name that expresses his eternal being. He wants you to know his name. And you say it all the time. Every time you say hallelujah, you say praise, Yahweh. This translation, for that and a number of reasons, is a priceless treasure—an amazing effort.[4]

The King James Bible usually translated Jehovah as "the LORD." That rendering is correct. The LSB changes the translation of the Hebrew (Jehovah) from "the LORD" to "Yahweh." Isaiah 40:3 is an example.

| AV | LSB |
|---|---|
| The voice of him that crieth in the wilderness, Prepare ye the way of **the LORD**, make straight in the desert a highway for our God. (Isaiah 40:3 AV) | A voice is calling, "Prepare the way for **Yahweh** in the wilderness; Make smooth in the desert a highway for our God." (Isaiah 40:3 LSB) |

God's inspired word in Mark 1:3 is evidence that "the LORD" is a correct rendering of the Hebrew (Jehovah). Mark 1:3 is a quote from the prophecy of Isaiah 40:3 regarding the coming of the Lord. "The voice of one crying in the wilderness, Prepare ye the way of **the Lord**, make his paths straight." (Mark 1:3 AV) It identifies Jesus Christ as "the Lord," the the eternal God, Jehovah. When the LSB renders the Mark 1:3 passage, is a quote from Isaiah 40:3, it follows the correct rendering of "the Lord." just as it is in the KJV.

THE VOICE OF ONE CRYING IN THE WILDERNESS, 'MAKE READY THE WAY OF **THE LORD**, MAKE HIS PATHS STRAIGHT.' (Mark 1:3 LSB)

If John MacArthur and the LSB were to be consistent, they would have rendered the quoted passage from Isiah 4:3 in Mark 1:3 as "Yahweh." The fact that they rendered Mark 1:3 as "the Lord" impeaches their avowed fidelity to the original Hebrew and undermines their claim that Yahweh is the correct translation of the Hebrew tetragrammaton, YHVH. The LSB translators know it would be wrong to render "the Lord" in Mark 1:3 as "Yahweh." But they fail to understand that it is just as wrong to render "the LORD" in Isaiah 40:3 and Jehovah in Exodus 6:2-3 as "Yahweh."

The translators of the LSB have gone on record to say that the KJV is wrong. They claim that "Jehovah we do believe is an incorrect way of pronouncing it [the tetragrammaton, YHVH]. But what that is, it is a misreading of the vowels that appear on the letters YHWH on the word Yahweh."[5] The LSB translators criticize God's word in the KJV; they speak evil of the way of truth. That is a sign that they are among the pernicious false teachers who would privily sneak into the church bringing damnable heresies about whom Peter warned us in 2 Peter 2:1-2. Peter said, "many shall follow their pernicious ways; by reason of whom **the way of truth shall be evil spoken of.**" *Id.*

# 2 Malignant Growth From Hebrew Roots

The rising popularity of the Hebrew Roots movement has spearheaded the recent upsurge in substituting Jehovah with Yahweh. The Hebrew Roots movement is a Zionist theology followed by Gentiles that emphasizes recovering Jewish legalism while claiming faith in Jesus. It is sometimes also called the Sacred Name movement. While those in the Hebrew Roots movement claim faith in Jesus, they have a different Jesus from the Biblical Jesus. There is no indication that James White or John MacArthur are part of the Hebrew Roots movement. But their adoption of Yahweh is an indication of how portions of the Hebrew Roots theology are wafting into the ersatz "Christian" churches.

Unsurprisingly, the Bible for the Hebrew roots movement, the Hebraic Roots Bible, substituted YAHWEH in every instance where the Hebrew word for JEHOVAH appears. Psalms 83:18 is one example.

| **AV** | **Hebraic Roots Bible** |
|---|---|
| That men may know that thou, whose name alone is **JEHOVAH**, art the most high over all the earth. (Psalms 83:18 AV) | And let them know you; that Your name is **YAHWEH**, and all life comes from you, the Most High over all the earth. (Psalms 83:18 Hebraic Roots Bible) |

The Hebrew consonant letters that have been translated Jehovah in English are often called the Tetragrammaton with the Hebrew letters *yod-hey-vav-hey* (ה ו ה י) (YHVH). The 'Y" in Hebrew takes on the "J" sound in English. There is no letter "J" in Hebrew. And the English alphabet did not have the letter "J" until the 16th century. But that does not mean that English did not have the "J" sound in their words. Prior to the 16th century the English letter "I" was used for both the "I" sound and the "J" sound. Indeed, in the 1611 King James Bible, you will find that Jesus was spelled "Iesus," but "Iesus" was pronounced as "Jesus."

It was during the 16th century that the letter "J" was introduced to distinguish the "I" sound from the "J" sound in English. The Tyndale Bible, published in 1525, used "J."[6] But that convention had not completely taken hold because the 1568 Bishops' Bible and the 1611 King James Bible used "I" for the "J" sound.

The English "J" sound in Hebrew is represented by the letter *yod* (י), which is written as "Y" in English. Indeed, check out the Old testament Hebrew for Jerusalem. It is "Yeruwshalaim," but no English speaker uses the soft "Y" sound to pronounce Jerusalem.

Psalms 119:73 in the KJV presents the Hebrew letter *yod* (י), but lists it as *jod*. That indicates that the Hebrew letter *yod* (י)

takes on the "j" sound in English. By rendering the Hebrew letter *yod* (ʼ) as *Jod* in Englsih, God's inspired word in English instructs us that the Hebrew letter *yod* (ʼ) takes on the "j" sound when translated into English.

The King James translators knew how to translate the Hebrew into English. Forty-seven renowned experts in all languages translated the King James Bible. The translators' expertise in ancient and modern languages was unparalleled in history. For example, one of the KJV translators, Lancelot Andrews, was fluent in fifteen modern languages and six ancient languages. He had an encyclopedic knowledge of scripture and was gifted with a photographic memory. So esteemed was he as a linguist and scholar that Hugo Grotius, the great Dutch legal authority and historian, called meeting Andrews "one of the special attractions of a visit to England."[7]

Lancelot Andrews was joined by Dr. Miles Smith, an expert in rabbinical learning and well-versed in Hebrew, Chaldee, Syriac, and Arabic. He was often called a "walking library."[8] Another KJV translator, John Bois, could write Hebrew elegantly at six years old. They collaborated with other renowned Hebraists, including, but not limited to, Edward Lively, Laurence Chaderton, Francis Dillingham, Thomas Harrison, John Richardson, and Robert Spaulding. These men were divided among six different companies of translators. The members of each company reviewed each other's work. And the work of each company was also reviewed by every other company. Thus, every member of every company was a translator of the whole.[9] The learning and piety of the scholars who worked on the King James Bible puts to shame the sophomoric language skills of those who act as translators of the modern profane Bibles.

Dr. John Hinton, who is a Hebrew language expert, addresses the issue of those that erroneously insist that the Hebrew letter *yod* (a.k.a., *jod*) (Y) should always be pronounced in English

10

as a soft "Y" rather than a hard "J." Dr. Hinton states:

> This is such an utterly silly and ignorant criticism that I find it embarrassing that there are actually Christians that present it as an argument. ... Y becomes a J in every name in English, French, and Spanish. In English the J is pronounced like J in Japan, while in French it is pronounced like S in pleasure, in Spanish it is pronounced like an H, in German it is pronounced like Y. This is a phonological and orthographical issue, not a theological one. There is no theological issue at stake in how one language interprets a certain phoneme. In every case of a name in Hebrew that begins with a *yod* (Y) it is pronounced with the appropriate phoneme for that language. This came about through phonological and orthographical changes in the developments of those languages. Even Hebrew itself went through huge phonological and orthographical changes in its long history. God's name is not a magic word to be chanted for power as the name cult seems to suggest for both the names of God and Jesus. My name [John] comes from a Hebrew word meaning given by God, which begins with a Y in Hebrew. It is Jean (zhan) in French, Juan (hwan) in Spanish, Giovanni in Italian, Hans in German, Yani in modern Greek, Ivan (eevan) in Russian, Yahya or Hanna (with a heavy H) in Arabic, and other variations exist in other languages. They all translate as John and I have no trouble adapting to any of them within the respective cultures and there is no reason for me to be insulted by any of these names. On the other hand, being addressed by a made up name based on a pagan deity would insult me.

If these name cultists find the J so objectionable, why don't they refer to Elijah as Elaiyah, Jeramiah as Yeramaiyah, Jacob as Yakov, Jonathan as Yanatan, Jerusalem as Yerushaleem, and so forth. For that matter why don't they use the Hebrew pronunciation for all of the names in the Bible, such as Dahveed, Moshe (Moses), Shmu'el (Samuel), Sha'ul (Saul), Shlomo (Solomon), and so forth, if they consider the issue to be so important. Since those who call God by a name that is not even Hebrew at all, and since they do so without a scrap of evidence to override the very solid evidence to the contrary, why do they have any constraints at all about inventing whimsical pointings for other names in the Bible?

\*\*\*

"The sound of the Hebrew letter jod came into English as the letter 'I,' used as a consonant and having the soft 'g' sound, like today's 'j.' In the past the letter 'I' was used as both a vowel (i) sound and as the consonant 'j' sound. The OED says that the sound of 'j,' though originally printed as 'I,' was pronounced as a soft 'g' (Oxford English Dictionary, Unabridged, 2nd Edition, Oxford: Clarendon Press, 1991, s.v. J). The 'JE' sound in JEHOVAH was spelled 'IE' and pronounced as 'JE.' To distinguish the consonant sound (soft 'g') of the letter 'I' from the vowel sound of 'I,' many scribes in the 1200s began putting a tail on the soft 'g' 'I,' making it look like our modern 'J.' The Spanish, in the 1500s, were the first to more consistently try to distinguish the consonant I (soft 'g') sound as the shape of a 'J.' At that same time English printers used 'J' and 'I' fonts interchangeably. ... During the 1600s, most languages began consistently using the extended 'I' form, now called a 'J,' to represent the 'j' (soft 'g') sound." [quoted in Riplinger, p. 418][10]

The Hebrew consonant letters for Jehovah are יהוה. Those Hebrew letters are read from right to left; their English representations are written from left to right (YHVH). The Hebrew letters י ה ו ה (YHVH) are only the consonant Hebrew letters without the vowel points. I will discuss the vowel points and their significance below. Hebrew words are read from right to left. And so *yod* (י) (Y or J), the tenth letter of the Hebrew alphabet is on the far right, followed by *hah* (ה) (H), the fifth letter of the Hebrew alphabet, followed by *vav* (ו) (V), which is the sixth letter of the Hebrew alphabet, and concluding with *hah* (ה) (H) again at the far left. It is commonly represented as YHVH; in Engish, it would be transliterated JHVH.

The Tetragrammaton (י ה ו ה) (YHVH or JHVH) is properly translated into English as JEHOVAH. And it would be properly pronounced as Jehovah in Englsih. The Hebrew letter *yod* (י), which is more correctly called *jod* in English (see Psalms 119:73 in the AV) takes on the "j" sound in English. And so words that begin with *yod* take on the constant "j" sound, like Jerusalem, Joseph, and Jehovah, which all start with *yod* (י) (a.ka., *jod*).

יהוה
YHVH

The next letter in the Tetragrammaton is *hah* (ה), which takes on the "h" sound in English. That is followed by the next letter in the Tetragrammatan, *vav* (ו), which takes on the consonant sound "v" in English. That is followed by *hah* (ה) as the last letter. When you look at Psalms 119 in the AV you will find the Hebrew alphabet listed in order. At Psalms 119:73 you will find *yod* listed as *jod* (י) in the AV. That means that *yod* takes on a hard consonant "j" sound (as in *jod*) in the inspired English word of God.

It is essential for English speakers reading an English Bible to understand the name of God in English correctly because when you read Exodus 6:2-3, you will realize that God was speaking to Moses. God was telling Moses his name in an audible voice. It is, therefore, important to accurately understand the truth of what God said. If God said his name is "Jehovah," which is how it is translated into English, then his name should be Jehovah in English.

E.W. Bullinger explains, "Jehovah means the Eternal, the Immutable One, He Who WAS, and IS, and IS TO COME. The Divine definition is given in Genesis 21:33."[11] (all capital letters in original) Nick Sayers explains: "In other words, God had appeared to Abraham, Isaac, and Jacob but not as 'the Eternal, Immutable One.' but as 'God Almighty.' But when God appeared to Moses, He made Himself known as Who He is, His very essence, i.e. Eternal."[12] Jesus is identified as Jehovah. The very name of Jesus means "Jehovah is salvation." Jesus stated: "I am Alpha and Omega, the beginning and the ending, saith the Lord, which is, and which was, and which is to come, the Almighty." Revelation 1:8. In that verse, we see that Jesus is thus revealing that he is Jehovah (i.e., the eternal God, who was, and is, and is to come). Is Yahweh, the Lord, which is, and which was, and which is to come, the Almighty? No! We will find out that Yahweh is the Midianite weather god.[13]

Later, when Moses penned Genesis, he used the word Jehovah to refer to the LORD. "These are the generations of the heavens and of the earth when they were created, in the day that the LORD [Jehovah] God made the earth and the heavens," (Genesis 2:4 AV)

But the heathen Schaff-Herzog Encyclopedia of Religious

14

Knowledge undermines the eternal and sovereign deity of Jehovah and claims he is instead Yahweh, a heathen god worshiped by the nomadic Midianites:

> Yahweh appears as an old deity of Sinai, revered in untold antiquity as a weather god, and as such brought by Moses to Israel, to him revealed through his connection with the Midianite priestly family.[14]

Thus, the Schaff-Herzog Encyclopedia acknowledges that their rendition of YHVH as "Yahweh" is based on the encyclopedia writers' belief that the Jews worshipped a heathen weather god of Sinai called Yahweh. The encyclopedia writers have a preconceived idea that serves to undermine the divinity of Jehovah. The encyclopedia then claims that "the form was never pronounced as Yehovah (Jehovah)."[15] But the writers of the encyclopedia offer no evidence to support their claims. Indeed, the encyclopedia is full of conjecture and qualifying statements like "it is supposed" and "the hypothesis of the Yahweh cult" and "it is highly improbable" and "rich harvest of suggestion of Yahweh" and "indications suggest." The entire entry is full of suppositions and guesses. The writers were just making things up. It is not scholarship. It is false progpaganda. Indeed, their "the hypothesis of the Yahweh cult" is based on mere possibility. The encyclopedia entry says so.

> There remains the **possibility** that in the time before Moses a part of the people dwelt near Sinai and that by this part Yahweh was worshiped and that from it Moses learned of him.[16]

They have grafted the heathen god, Yahweh, in place of the Holy God, Jehovah. Historians state that Yahweh is one of the gods of the Syro-Palestinian pantheon, which included Baal. Heathen historians claim that Yahweh was adopted as a god by the

15

Jews from the surrounding tribes and eventually emerged as the national god of Israel and Judah.

James Miller and John Hayes reveal that "Yahwehism and Baalism existed alongside each other with essentially the same cultic procedures and paraphernalia."[17] The mythology of heathen historians is that it was later that Israel worshiped Yahweh as a monotheistic god.[18] What becomes clear is that Yahweh is not an alternative pronunciation of YHVH. What is happening is that infidel historians in service of Satan are replacing eternal God Almighty, Jehovah, with the heathen weather god, Yahweh. There is no new thing under the sun. *See* Ecclesiates 1:9. This is what the lying prophets of old did. They replaced God's name with Baal. God explains in Jeremiah:

> I have heard what the prophets said, that prophesy lies in my name, saying, I have dreamed, I have dreamed. How long shall this be in the heart of the prophets that prophesy lies? yea, they are prophets of the deceit of their own heart; **Which think to cause my people to forget my name by their dreams which they tell every man to his neighbour, as their fathers have forgotten my name for Baal.** (Jeremiah 23:25-27)

John King, the translator and editor of John Calvin's Commentary, cites the elaborate investigation of the origin and import of the name Jehovah by Ernst Wilhelm Hengstenberg (1802-1869), Professor Extraordinarius of Theology at Berlin. King discovered that Hengstenberg refuted the folklore of impious historians. He concluded that "[...] (Jehovah) ... was not derived from any heathen source whatever. Consequently, it is to be traced to 'a Hebrew etymology.'"[19]

Dr. Nehemia Gordon is a renowned Hebraist. He is a Karaite Jew who recognizes the written Tanakh (Old Testament) as the sole religious authority. Dr. Gordon tried to track down the source of the Hebrew vowels for Yahweh. He researched extensively, trying to find the authority for Yahweh as the Tetragrammaton (YHVH) pronunciation. What he found surprised him. There was no ancient authority for pronouncing the Tetragrammaton (YHVH) as Yahweh.

> What do we have in Jewish sources, and what do we have in Hebrew Bible manuscripts? There isn't a single Hebrew Bible manuscript that has Yahveh or Yahweh, nothing, nowhere, anywhere. There isn't a single Jewish source that has Yahweh. Let's say an ancient or medieval Jewish source.[20]

Dr. Gordon was trying to find authority for pronouncing the Tetragrammaton (YHVH) as Yahweh. He contacted authorities from the Hebrew Roots movement to find out their source for Yahweh. Astoundingly, they admitted that the vowels for Yahweh have no Hebrew manuscript authority. They said that they constructed Yahweh from an unpointed Hebrew text. That is a text with no vowels.

That means that the Hebrew Roots movement is just making it up. They just inserted the vowels as they saw fit into the consonants of the Tetragrammaton (YHVH) to come up with the name Yahweh. The Hebrew roots people are doing the very same thing that the apostate Jews did when they created the unpointed Hebrew text so that they could make a passage mean whatever they wanted it to mean and not be restricted by the pesky vowels. An unpointed Hebew text is virtually meaningless. An unpointed text allows a mischievous rabbi to give his private interpretation of what vowels to insert to give a verse its meaning. Dr. Gordon states:

> I didn't have any manuscripts so I wrote to these Christian folks or maybe Hebrew Roots folks, who

say Yahweh, and I say which vowels do I put in here? ... They said we don't use Hebrew vowels. Okay, but if it if you can't translate it into Hebrew, the Hebrew vowel system, then it has no meaning in Hebrew.[21]

# 3 The Mythology of Infidel Scholars

D r. Gordon cited 19 learned rabbis with eclectic backgrounds who, through history, all stated that Yehovah was the correct rendering of the Tetragrammaton (YHVH) in Hebrew. In Hebrew, it is pronounced Yehovah, whereas in English, it is pronounced Jehovah.

> Right now have 19 rabbis who explicitly say that the vowels of the name are Yehovah ... in Hebrew. ... You could say they're wrong. But what you can't say is this [Jehovah] is something that was invented by ignorant Christians because we have multiple rabbis, who, some of them were aware of what the Christians were saying others had no clue what the Christians were saying, and they all believed it was Jehovah. ... There is no Rabbi in historical sources who says it's Yahweh or Yahveh.[22]

Yehovah in Hebrew would be Jehovah in English. Dr. Gordon could not find any source for Yahweh as the pronunciation of the Tetragrammaton (יהוה) (YHVH) before the German linguist Wilhelm Gesenius (1786-1842) in his Hebrew lexicon. Gesenius was the progenitor of pronouncing the Tetragrammaton

(YHVH) as Yahweh.

Dr. Nehemia Gordon, Ph.D., researched the origins of Yahweh and was shocked to find out that Yahweh is not the God of the Bible, but is a pagan god worshipped by the Samaritans.[23] The Romans worshipped Jupiter as the principal god in their henotheistic mythology. Josephus reveals that the Samaritans rededicated their temple to Jupiter (a.k.a., Zeus) in 168 B.C. The Samaritans called Jupiter Yoveh. In Latin, Yoveh was pronounced Yoweh, which ultimately became Yahweh.

Dr. Gordon quotes from Wilhelm Gesenius (1786-1842). Gesenius' Hebrew Lexicon is the foundation of Hebrew biblical studies at Hebrew University today. Gesenius championed the use of Yahweh as the name of God. Gesenius, in his Hebrew and Chaldee Lexicon of the Old Testament Scriptures, states: "I suppose this word [Yahweh] to be one of the most remote antiquity, perhaps of the same origin as Jovis, Jupiter, and transferred from the Egyptians to the Hebrews."[24]

Gesenius, the most authoritative advocate for YHVH being pronounced Yahweh instead of Jehovah, let the cat out of the bag. He confirmed that Yahweh, the name he championed as the name of the God who communed with Moses, was the name of a heathen god originating in Egypt. That was too much information. Some infidel scholars wanted to introduce Yahweh in place of Jehovah, and they did not like it to be known (at least at the outset) that Yahweh was a heathen god.

One infidel scholar realized that something had to be done to undermine Gesenius's statement. Enter Samuel Prideaux Tregelles (1813-1875). Tregelles was a member of the English revision committee for the abominable Revised Version of the Bible. After Gesenius' death, Tregelles became the editor of Gesenius' lexicon. In that capacity, Tregelles took the opportunity to put brackets in a later edition of Gesenius' lexicon alleging that

Gesenius retracted his statement about the heathen origins of Yahweh.[25]

But the alleged statement of retraction sounds nothing like a retraction. In the alleged retraction, Gesenius referred to studies into derivations a "waste of time and labour." That is not the same as saying that what he found in his analysis of the derivation of Yahweh was incorrect. Of course, there are infidels like Tragelles who are interested in undermining Gesenius's statement and would desire that Gesenius would retract his finding of the heathen origins of Yahweh. Such a finding of the heathen origins of Yahweh by someone as esteemed as Gesenius, who championed the name, Yahweh, would be a damning indictment against using Yahweh to refer to God. And that is what Tragelles argued against. Tragelles said: "What an idea! God himself revealed this [Yahewh] as his own name; the Israelites could never have received it from the Egyptians."[26] Tragelles has an interest in undermining evidence of the heathen origins of Yahweh. He wants people to think that YHVH should be translated as Yahweh. After examining the evidence, Dr. Gordon concluded that Yahweh is NOT another way to pronounce Jehovah, the Tetragrammaton (YHVH), but is, in fact, a pagan deity, just as Gesenius revealed.[27]

Yahweh is not Jehovah. Modern scholars have confirmed what Gesenius revealed about the origins of Yahweh as a heathen god. They have taken up Gesenius's torch and argue, as he did, that YHVH (יהוה) is not the eternal God, Jehovah, but is instead a heathen god, Yahweh. For example, Daniel E. Fleming, Ph.D., researched the origin of Yahweh and determined it is the name of a heathen god. He has alleged that the heathen god, Yahweh, was absorbed and worshipped by the Jews. Dr. Fleming is the Ethel and Irvin A. Edelman Professor of Hebrew and Judaic Studies at New York University. Fleming is the author of many scholarly books.

In Fleming's book *Yahweh before Israel: Glimpses of*

*History in a Divine Name*, he opines that Yahweh is not the name of the eternal God of heaven. Fleming researched the origins of Yahweh. He found reference to Yahweh in ancient Egyptian hieroglyphics. He states that the name, Yhw3, pronounced "Yahweh" originated as the name of of a nomadic people of Shasu-land that eventually became the name of a heathen god, Yahweh. He argues that the heathen god, Yahweh, was then adopted by the Jews during their sojourn in the desert after God rescued them from their Egyptian captivity.

Fleming opines that that Yhw3 of Shasu-land was a people, and that name became later the god Yahweh. He opined that "the people understood themselves to have as a divine patron a god so fully identified with them as to share their name."[28]

Prof. Israel Knohl. Ph.D., is the Yehezkel Kaufmann Professor of Bible at the Hebrew University of Jerusalem and a senior research fellow at the Shalom Hartman Institute. He holds a Ph.D. in Bible from Hebrew University. Knohl has written numerous highly aclaimed academic publications. Knohl mostly agrees with Dr. Fleming.

Dr. Fleming promotes a Shasu origin for Yahweh, which arguably excludes Midianites as the origin. But Dr. Knohl argues that while it was in the land of Shasu where the Jews adopted Yahweh, it was under the influence of the Midianites. Dr. Knohl states that "It thus appears that the Hebrews adopted the Midianite deity YHW or YHWH [Yahweh], whom they came to know in their stay in the area of Seir – Edom which is in "the land of Shasu YHW."[29] Dr. Knohl argues that YHWH is a heathen god, Yahweh, which was adopted by the Jews.

> But how did the deity YHW [Yahweh] become
> transformed into the God of Israel? ... It thus
> appears that the Hebrews adopted the Midianite
> deity YHW or YHWH, whom they came to know

in their stay in the area of Seir – Edom which is in "the land of Shasu YHW."[30]

Unsurprisingly, the New International Version (NIV) Bible publishers have taken the position that "the majority opinion today is that 'Yahweh' is the original pronunciation"[31] of the tetragrammaton, YHWH. The NIV writes the tetragrammaton YHWH instead of YHVH because it more closely comports with its mythology that the tetragrammaton is pronounced, "Yahweh." The NIV wants to migrate people toward the worship of the heathen god, Yahweh.

# 4 Yahweh Is an Erroneous Translation

One clue that Yahweh and Jehovah are not the same is that they carry two different meanings. Hebraist Dr. Nehemia Gordon, Ph.D., explains that Jehovah literally means He who was, He who is, and He who will be.[32] Dr. Israel Knohl explains that Yahweh has an entirely different meaning. He states:

> God reveals his name to Moses as "I am" from the Hebrew root, "being." The name YHWH, [Yahweh] however, originates in Midian, and derives from the Arabic term for "love, desire, or passion." ... [T]he name of Yahweh means Impassioned. It reflects Yahweh's passionate love for his worshipers.[33]

Yahweh and Jehovah carry two different meanings because Yahweh is NOT Jehovah. Jehovah is the eternal God of heaven, who was, who is, and who will be. In contrast, Yahweh is a heathen god of passion.

How did they change the *vav* (ו), which has a hard "v" sound to the soft w in Yahweh? It was started with the apostate Germans who wrote "w," for the hard "v" sound in the German language. The Schaff–Herzog Encyclopedia of Religious Knowledge was based on an earlier German encyclopedia, the *Realencyklopädie für protestantische Theologie und Kirche*. When transliterating from German to English, many English speakers often miss that the German "w" is pronounced as the English "v." For example, the German Wagner would pronounced by a German as "Vagner," although it would still be spelled Wagner. What an English speaker would call wiener schnitzel with a soft "w"sound a German would call "veiner schnitzel" with a hard "v" sound. But the German spelling would remain as wiener schnitzel; the w would take on the "v" sound. When the German was transliterated into English, the English speakers read the "w" not as a hard "v" sound but as a soft "w" sound. That soft English "w" has given rise to the change causing the erroneous "weh" sound in Yahweh. Dr. John Hinton, Ph.D., states that "the Hebrew *vav* is pronounced as V not W. This error came about due to the misreading of German Hebrew grammars, which use W for the English V."[34] Gail Riplinger explains:

> Where did the phony 'weh' sound in Yahweh come from? As Green said, "German sources." In German "the "v" sound is rendered by the "double u" ("w"). Although the German critics spelled the name Yahweh, they pronounced it, Yahveh. ... Because Germans use the letter 'w' for the 'v' sound, those reading or translating German theological works have brought in the German letter 'w' for 'v.' It is not to be pronounced like an English 'w,' but like a 'v.'[35]

Changing what God said his name is (Jehovah) to Yahweh is changing what God said. Yahweh is not at all Jehovah. Yahweh is a heathen god. And the original promoters of Yahweh say so. God has commanded us not to even mention the names of other gods. Imagine his dipleasure against those who would change his scriptures to replace his name "Jehovah" with a heathen god,

"Yahweh."

> And in all things that I have said unto you be circumspect: and make no mention of the name of other gods, neither let it be heard out of thy mouth. (Exodus 23:13 AV)

This modern trend of pronouncing the Tetragrammaton as Yahweh began in Germany. Gail Riplinger explains:

> In the 19th century, as unbelieving German critics of the Bible were hammering away at the word of God, they tried to refashion God's name, JEHOVAH. They asserted that the God of Israel's name should be pronounced Yahweh because, to them, he was nothing more than an offshoot of the pagan deity "Yaho."[36]

That corruption by the German liberals was a deviation from the traditional translation of YHVH as Jehovah. Gail Riplinger reveals:

> In his scholarly book, *A Dissertation Concerning the Antiquity of the Hebrew Language, Letters, Vowel-Points and Accents*, John Gill (1697-1771), eminent theologian and writer, documents the use of the very name JEHOVAH from before 200 B.C. and throughout the centuries of the early church and the following millennium. ... Even commentators such as Nicholas of Lyra, Tostatus, Cajetan, and Bonfrere defended the pronunciation 'JEHOVAH' as received by Moses on Mt. Horeb. The name is found in the writings of Raymund Martin in the 1200s and Porchetus in the 1300s. Theodore Beza, Galatinus, and Cajetan, among many others, use it in the 1500s. Scholars such as

26

Michaelis, Drach and Stier proved the name as the original. The 1602 Spanish Bible uses the name Iehova and gave a lengthy defense of the pronunciation Jehovah in its preface. In "the 17th century the pronunciation JEHOVAH was zealously defended by Fuller, Gataker, Leusden and others.[37]

But the heathen servants of Satan got to it and sought to undermine Jehovah and replace him with their heathen god, Yahweh. Gail Riplinger elaborates:

> Genebrardus seems to have been the first to suggest the pronunciation Iahue [pronounced Yahweh], but it was not until the 19th century that it became generally accepted" (EB, pp. 311-314). Anti-Semitic German liberals, like Driver and Delitzsch, eagerly grasped the new pronunciation, Yahweh. They and other unsaved 'higher critics,' denied that the Old Testament was actually given by God. They grasped at any straw to shelter their unbelief, asserting that the Old Testament was the creation of men who adopted and adapted stories, words, and names from neighboring pagan religions and languages. The higher critics used the new pronunciation, Yahweh, as so-called proof that the God of Israel was nothing more than a tribal god, whose name had evolved from pagan gods like Yaho or Ya-ve, worshipped by the Babylonians and Canaanites, the Hebrews' captors and neighbors. They said, Yahweh "meant Destroyer."[38]

Dr. Hinton explains that the Hebrew text does not support the soft English "W". It is wrong to translate the Hebrew *vav* (ו) in English as "W."

Those who are opposed to the KJV and call God by name Yahweh are not only giving an erroneous pronunciation of his name according to the pointing of the text, but according to the pronunciation of the Hebrew itself. As Gail Riplinger astutely points out in her *[In] Awe of Thy Word*, the Hebrew *vav* is pronounced as V not W. This error came about due to the misreading of German Hebrew grammars, which use W for the English V (note: the German V is pronounced like the English F). If these Bible "correctors" want to ignore the Hebrew text and pronounce his name as suggested by 19th century atheistic mythologists, they should use the name Yahveh so that at least they would appear less ignorant. It always puzzled me to hear atheistic scholars at Harvard pronounce the name as Yahweh when the same scholars would always pronounce the *vav* as a V every other place that they use it. Apparently this perversion of his name has become so well established within the Bible-scoffing and Bible-correcting communities that even those who know better mispronounce even the perverted variation of his name. It confused me that they would pronounce it as if it were an Arabic word instead of Hebrew word until I understood the purpose of the corruption.[39]

Dr. Nehemia Gordon, Ph.D., is a Hebraist who has worked as a translator on the Dead Sea Scrolls and a researcher deciphering ancient Hebrew manuscripts.[40] He confirms the opinion of Dr. Hinton. Dr. Gordon states that the proper pronunciation of the Hebrew *vav* (ו) is with the hard "v" sound. He states that Arabic also has a *vav* (و), and it is pronounced as "wow" in Arabic because Arabic does not have a "va" sound. But Arabic is not Hebrew, and the Hebrew *vav* (ו) is pronounced with a hard

28

"v." Dr. Gordon states that the only Jews who pronounce the *vav* (ו) with a soft "w" sound are Jews in Arabic lands who are speaking Arabic.[41] The soft "w" sound is an Arabic pronunciation of *vav* (ו); it is not Hebrew. Thus, Yahweh is an incorrect pronunciation of YHVH (י ה ו ה).

Satan's minions have created a little deception. He has his own set of lying alleged Hebraists who claim that the historical pronunciation of *vav* (ו) is with a "w." Jeff A. Benner is an example. Benner is an adherent to the Hebrew Roots theology.[42] He claims first that the King James Bible is not the inspired word of God. He also claims that the Old Testament was written in an "Old Hebrew" that is different from the Hebrew we see today. Armed with his new, made-up Hebrew, Benner can argue that the original sound for *vav* in ancient Hebrew was a soft "w" and not the hard "v," as in modern Hebrew.

Jeff A. Benner has used his new reconstructed Hebrew phonics to claim that YHVH should be read as Yahweh and not JEHOVAH.[43] Dr. Nehehmia Gordon has completely impeached Benner and has proven that Benner's claim is wrong.[44] Regarding the letter *vav* (ו), Dr. Gordon explains that the proper pronunciation of the Hebrew *vav* (ו) is with the hard "v" sound. Dr. Gordon states that the claim that *vav* (ו) has ever been pronounced as "wow" is simply wrong. It is only in Arabic that *vav* (ו) is pronounced as "wow." Dr. Gordon proved that *vav* (ו) has always been pronounced as "v" in ancient and modern Hebrew. He demonstrated that fact with two words from the ancient Hebrew in Ezekiel.[45]

In the book of Ezekiel at 10:12, we find the Hebrew word *gav* (ג ב), meaning back(s). Reading the Hebrew word right to left, the second letter in that word is a *beyt* (ב). When *beyt* (ב) appears

29

at the end of the word it takes on the "v" sound, hence *gav*. In Ezekiel 23:35 we also find the Hebrew word *gav* (גו). But this time, the second letter is a *vav* (ו) which takes on the "v" sound because, again, the Hebrew word is *gav* (meaning back). These are two Hebrew words, both meaning "back." They are actually the same word, with the same pronunciation, "*gav*," meaning back. They are just spelled differently. But in Ezekiel 23:35, *gav* (back) is spelled using a *vav* (ו) as the second letter, which necessarily must take on the "v" sound to get "*gav*." The only way this would be possible is if the letter *vav* (ו) in the word *gav* (גו) is pronounced with a "v." Ezekiel was written circa 592 to 570 B.C. and would be ancient Hebrew. The Ezekiel passages containing *gav* with two different spellings with one containing a *vav* (ו) are proof that that *vav* (ו) has always taken on the "v" sound in Hebrew.

Put another way, the Hebrew word for "back" is *gav*. The second consonant sound at the end of *gav* is *beyt* (ב) in Ezekiel 10:12. *Beyt* takes on the "v" sound at the end of a Hebrew word. *Gav* (back) is always pronounced with a "v" sound. That fact is established beyond any doubt. When we read *gav*, meaning back, again in Ezekiel 23:35, this time spelled differently in Hebrew, with the second consonant letter *vav* (ו), it can only mean one thing. *Vav* (ו) takes on the "v" sound in Ezekiel 25:35. Ezekiel 10:12 rendering of *gav* confirms the Ezekiel rendering of *gav* in Ezekiel 23:35. That means that *vav* (ו) takes on the "v" sound in ancient Hebrew, just as in modern Hebrew.

Jeff A. Benner was unwilling to budge from his erroneous position when Dr. Gordon proved that *vav* (ו) has always taken on the "v" sound in ancient and modern Hebrew.[46] He realized that if he yielded that point his Hebrew Roots' house of cards would collapse. Benner's opinion is corrupted by his belief that the English AV Bible is not the inspired word of God and that God's name is Yahweh.[47] Benner has an agenda to maintain the myth that the original pronunciation for *vav* is "w" which is one of the keystones for the claim that God's name is Yahweh and not Jehovah.[48] Benner cares not for the truth.

# 5 The Jewish Fable of Unpointed Hebrew

S atan figured out a way to change Jehovah into Yahweh by removing the vowel points that locked in Jehovah as the name of God. Satan and his minions had to reduce the Hebrew scripture to only the consonants before they could fill in their own vowels. They started with YHVH. With the vowels gone, they could argue that YHVH means YAHWEH.

In order for that scheme to work, they needed to float a lie that the original Hebrew scriptures did not have vowel points. They claimed that the vowel points were added much later and were not part of the inspired scriptures. Hebrew script uses vowel points, which are small marks indicating vowels. On or about 1538 Elias Levita, a famous Jewish grammarian, floated a theory that the original Hebrew text did not have vowel points.[49] He theorized that the original Hebrew text was made up of only consonants. He claimed that the Masorites added vowel points based on the Jewish oral traditions to create the Hebrew Old Testament we know today. Levita's mythology, if true, would mean that the Hebrew Old Testament is uninspired because the words would only have meaning through the vowels supplied by the oral traditions of men rather than from prophets as they were moved by God. Invoking oral traditions is the very thing that Jesus criticized the Jews for doing.

> Howbeit in vain do they worship me, teaching for doctrines the commandments of men. **For laying aside the commandment of God, ye hold the tradition of men,** as the washing of pots and cups: and many other such like things ye do. And he said unto them, Full well **ye reject the commandment of God, that ye may keep your own tradition.** (Mark 7:7-9 AV)

In contrast, God states that the holy scriptures are not subject to the will of man or the private interpretation of the Masoretes or anyone else. All scripture was given to men as the Holy Ghost moved them.

> Knowing this first, that no prophecy of the scripture is of any private interpretation. For the prophecy came not in old time by the will of man: but holy men of God spake as they were moved by the Holy Ghost." (2 Peter 1:20-21 AV)

Did the Hebrew original scripture have vowels? Yes they did. The modern popular deception that the original Hebrew scriptures had no vowels is a lie constructed by Jews and their fellow travelers who want to conceal the prophecies about Jesus Christ and undermine the authority of God. The Jews removed the points that indicated vowel sounds in the scripture they used in their synagogues so that they could then reconstruct a phony scripture to conceal the deity of Jesus Christ.

Vowels in Hebrew are represented by marks called points. Hebraist Dr. Nehemia Gordon did extensive research into ancient Hebrew texts and found that the vowel points for the Tetragrammaton (יהוה) (YHVH) always have been *sheva, holem,* and *kamatz.*[50] Thus, the English pronunciation of the pointed

Tetragrammaton (YHVH) can only be Jehovah. He concluded that the Tetragrammaton (YHVH) pronunciation cannot be Yahweh. Indeed, Dr. Gordon determined that the Tetragrammaton (YHVH) pronunciation in Hebrew has always been Yehovah (in English, it would be pronounced Jehovah). Dr. Gordon uncovered more than 1.000 ancient Hebrew Bible manuscripts containing the vowel points that render the Tetragrammaton (YHVH) in Hebrew as Yehovah; in English it would be pronounced Jehovah.[51]

Below are two representations of the Tetragrammaton (YHVH or JHVH) (יהוה). The one on the left is without any vowel points and the one on the right is pointed with vowels. The pointed version of the Tetragrammaton was the Hebrew text from which the AV English was translated.

יהוה          יְהֹוָה

**YHVH Without Vowel Points**          **JEHOVAH With Vowel Points**

In the graphic below, you can see how the different vowel points lock in the word Jehovah. Recall that you must read Hebrew from right to left. The consonant are *yod* (י), on the far right, followed by *hah* (ה), followed by *vav* (ו), and concluding with *hah* (ה) again at the far left. When translated into English with the vowel points the word is Jehovah. With the vowel points, it is impossible to translate YHVH as Yahweh.

יְהֹוָה

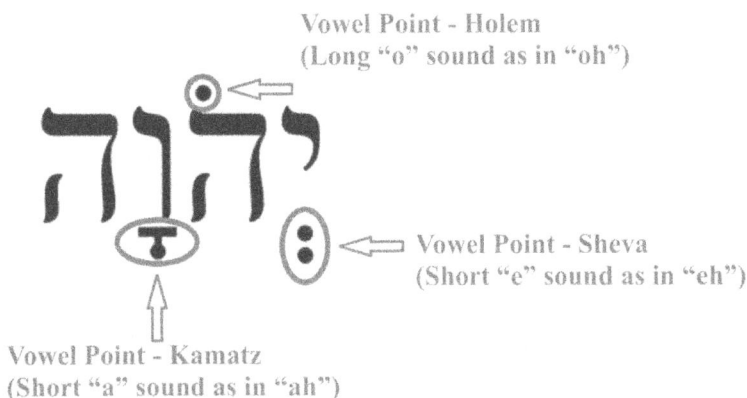

Above is the Hebrew word for JEHOVAH reading right to left. The vowels are indicated by the circled points. The consonants are, from right to left, *yod* (י) (J), *hah* (ה) (H), *vav* (ו) (V), and *hah* (ה) (H).

John Gill (1697-1771) traced the authenticity of the Hebrew Bible's vowel points back through the centuries to Moses.[52] His extensive research proves that the Hebrew Bible was written with vowel points. Gill found that the claim that vowel points were added by the Masoretes around 1000 A.D. is a myth that does not stand up to the historical evidence.

Not only that, but God himself informs us that the Hebrew scriptures were written with vowel points. Jesus stated: "For verily I say unto you, Till heaven and earth pass, **one jot or one tittle** shall in no wise pass from the law, till all be fulfilled." (Matthew 5:18 AV) A jot is "the least part of anything."[53] A tittle is a "small stroke or point in writing."[54] It is "[a] dot or other small mark used as a diacritic."[55] A diacritic is "a sign placed above or below a character or letter to indicate that it has a different phonetic value, is stressed, or for some other reason."[56] That is precisely what is done in Hebrew with the vowel points.

The jots and titles to which Jesus referred are an allusion to the diacritical marks used in Hebrew to designate the vowel sounds. Jesus was speaking about "the law," which is a reference to the law as it appeared in the Hebrew scriptures. That indicates that the original Hebrew scriptures had vowel points. That passage in Matthew 5:18 impeaches the claim that the vowel points were a later emendation made by men to the inspired Hebrew scriptures. The vowel points were, in fact, there from the beginning. And that is precisely what John Gill found in his extensive research.

Unpointed Hebrew Old Testament texts (Jews call it the Tanakh) have been constructed by Jews in order to have text that allows for wider interpretation and manipulation. Gill stated that without any points (vowels) a combination of consonants could be used to create up to ten different words. John Gill explains:

> There are other reasons why unpointed copies are kept and used in the synagogues of the Jews. They may help us to ascertain the origin of this custom and the reason for its continuance. One reason that the Cabalists, and those who interpreted the scriptures allegorically, might have the opportunity of establishing their own various senses of them. An unpointed Bible will do this, but a pointed Bible will not. ... This is what R. Bechai plainly suggested was the original cause and reason for using unpointed copies: "Letters which are not pointed give various senses. They are divided into various meanings. Because of this we are commanded not to point the book of the law because the literal sense of every word is according to the punctuation. There is only one literal sense in a pointed word, but an unpointed word a man may understand many ways and find out many wonderful and excellent things."[57]

Armed with the unpointed text, the Jews could rewrite the scriptures to their liking. Of course, that is not new for the Jews.

They are repeat offenders. In Mark 7:7-9, Jesus explained how the Jews laid aside the commandments of God so that they could hold the traditions of men. They rejected the commandments of God to follow their own traditions.

Gill concluded that a particular motivation for the Jews to remove the vowel points was to change the meaning of passages in the Bible. For example, we find in the Chabad: The Complete Jewish Bible that in Isaiah 9:6, they removed the prophecy regarding the birth of Jesus Christ, who is to be called the "Wonderful, Counsellor, The mighty God, The everlasting Father, The Prince of Peace." They replace it with a passage where God calls a child "the prince of peace." That corrupted passage in the Jewish Bible removes the eternal deity of Christ as the "Wonderful, Counsellor, The mighty God, The everlasting Father." Note that the Chabad Complete Jewish Bible is missing the verse at Isaiah 9:1 and so Isaiah 9:6 is numbered Isaiah 9:5 in the Chabad Complete Jewish Bible.

| AV | Chabad Jewish Bible |
|---|---|
| For unto us a child is born, unto us a son is given: and the government shall be upon his shoulder: and **his name shall be called Wonderful, Counsellor, The mighty God, The everlasting Father, The Prince of Peace.** (Isaiah 9:6 AV) | For a child has been born to us, a son given to us, and the authority is upon his shoulder, and **the wondrous adviser, the mighty God, the everlasting Father, called his name, "the prince of peace."** Isaiah 9:5 (Isaiah 9:6 in Englsih Bibles) Chabad: The Complete Jewish Bible. |

All one need do is read the Bible and it becomes clear that the Hebrew scriptures were written with vowel points. For instance, in Deuteronomy 27:8, God commands: "And thou shalt write upon the stones all the **words** of this law very **plainly**." How

37

were the Jews to write plainly all the words of God's law without using vowel points. There is no way to be faithful to God's commands by only using consonants and no vowels. Such initialisms would not even be "words." And they would not be written "very plainly." Such a text would be obfuscation.

Indeed, a text made up only of consonants contains no words. Each series of consonants would be an initialism. Words require vowels. Indeed, you cannot even say the consonant letters without adding a vowel. For example, the English letter "b" is pronounced "be" and the English letter "v" is pronounced "ve." A series of consonants without vowels becomes a meaningless initialism. The string of consonants can only be given meaning by adding vowels.

We know the Old Testament had vowel points because God states that the "**words** of the LORD are pure words." Psalm 12:6. He has promised to keep and preserve his "**words**" from "this generation for ever." Psalms 12:7. Jesus promised that "Heaven and earth shall pass away, but my **words** shall not pass away." Matthew 24:35. Consonants without vowels are initialisms. Initialisms are not words. God did not give us initialisms in the Old Testament. He gave us his **words**. It is a lie that the original Hebrew Old Testament did not have vowel pointings. Notice that throughout scripture, God identifies his **words** being spoken. Consonants with no vowels are not **words** that can be spoken.

> As for me, this is my covenant with them, saith the LORD; My spirit that is upon thee, and my **words** which I have **put in thy mouth**, shall not depart **out of thy mouth**, nor **out of the mouth of thy seed**, nor **out of the mouth of thy seed's seed,** saith the LORD, from henceforth and for ever. (Isaiah 59:21 AV)

The Roman Catholic Church could not be happier with

Levita's new theory of an unpointed Hebrew Old Testament. Thoms Ross explains:

> The idea of the recent addition of the points was popular among the Catholics, for it lent support to their idea of the superiority of the Latin Vulgate to the Hebrew (and Greek) original, formally canonized in the Council of Trent, and became a tool in anti-Protestant polemic, for the ambiguity which resulted from the removal of the points mitigated the Reformers' doctrine of the perspicuity of Scripture and supported the Romanist contention for the necessity of infallible interpretation by their organization.[58]

John Morinus (1591-1659), a Catholic convert from Protestantism, represents a typical counter-reformation apologetic that the resulting ambiguities in the unpointed Hebrew scriptures elevated the Roman Catholic priesthood to prominence in interpreting the meaning of the Bible.

> The reason why God ordained the Scriptures to be written in this ambiguous manner [without points] is because it was His will that every man should be subject to the Judgment of the Church, and not interpret the Bible in his own way. For seeing that the reading of the Bible is so difficult, and so liable to various ambiguities, from the very nature of the thing, it is plan that it is not the will of God that every one should rashly and irreverently take upon himself to explain it; nor to suffer the common people to expound it at their pleasure; but that in those things, as in other matters respecting religion, it is His will that the people should depend upon the priests.[59]

In 1748, Hebraist Peter Whitfield soundly debunked the myth constructed by Elias Levita that the vowel points were later emendations by the Masoretes.[60] Whitfield proved, through historical evidence and scripture itself, that Levita's claim was impossible. He gives many examples where the same consonants with different points create different words and, thus, entirely different meanings. Dr. Thomas Strouse of Emanual Baptist Seminary reviewed Whitfield's work and concluded that Whitfield was correct. He agrees with Whitfield that "Scripture is based on words and words are based on consonants and vowels. If there are no vowels in the Hebrew OT originals, then there is no Divine authority of the Hebrew OT Scriptures." [61] Dr. Strouse added his own analysis of why it is impossible for the inspired Hebrew Old Testament to have been written without Hebrew vowel points.

> When the Lord renewed His covenant with Israel, He used Moses to write the very same words that were on the initial tablets (Ex. 34:1 ff.). The Lord said to Moses, "Write thou these words: for after the tenor of these words I have made a covenant with thee and with Israel" (v. 27). The expression "after the tenor of these words" (`al piy hadevariym ha'elleh) could be translated literally "on [the basis of] the mouth of these words." The only way Moses could have written the Lord's spoken words was to hear the vowels in the consonants and then to write the words with the vowels intact. The Mosaic Law, then, constituted the very written words of Jehovah, including the consonants and vowels. Furthermore, the Jews were to obey the Mosaic Law in minute detail, not adding to nor diminishing from it (Dt. 4:2). They were to keep or preserve (shamar) the Law and not forget the things they had seen and were written down in it, and then to teach their children the Mosaic Law (vv. 6, 9, 10; cf. 6:7; 32:46). These

verses conclusively argue against any notion that the vowel sounds were merely given to Moses who passed on the oral tradition of the pronunciation until the Masoretes invented a system to approximate the vowels. Levitas' speculation that the Masoretes invented the points has nothing to commend it but has all Scriptural authority to condemn it.[62]

Dr. Strouse states that God's commending one who meditates on his law would be meaningless without vowel points.

> The initial Psalm addresses the blessed man and his responsibility to delight in and meditate on the law of the Lord, stating: "But his delight is in the law of the LORD; and in his law doth he meditate day and night"(Ps. 1:2). The word "meditate" comes from hagah that means "to mutter" and suggests the deliberate pronunciation of the words of Scripture. It is impossible to recite consonants without vowels and it is impossible to delight (*chaphatz*) in consonants with non-authoritative vowels. Again, the fallacious view that man invented the Hebrew vowel points has nothing to commend it. Is there any reason that Bible believers must countenance the view that the Lord God, the Creator of language, disdains vowels, at least to the extent that He would preserve them in written form? After all, has not the Lord Jesus Christ referred to Himself as the *Alpha* and *Omega* (Rev. 1:8; 21:6), the first and last vowels of the Greek language?[63]

The brilliant linguist John Owen (1616-1683), whom many view as the greatest British theologian of the 17th century,[64] disproved Levita's claim. Owen was fluent in Greek, Latin, and

Hebrew. His mastery of those languages is apparent in his writings. For example, in his book *The Devine Origin of Scripture,*[65] Owen segued from English to Greek to Latin to Hebrew with aplomb and adroitness. Owen concluded that the scriptural and historical evidence proves that the original Hebrew scriptures were pointed.

Owen averred that the Hebrew points in the holy scriptures were of utmost importance because "[v]owels are the life of words; consonants without them are dead and immovable."[66] Owen favorably quoted Hebraist Radulphus Cevallerius who opined that having an unpointed Hebrew text of scripture is to pluck up the scripture by the roots "for without the vowels and notes of distinction it hath nothing firm and certain."[67] Owen also favorably quoted Professor of Hebrew Johannes Isaac (1515-1557): "He that reads the Scriptures without points is like a man that rides a horse without a bridle; he may be carried he knows not whither."[68] An unpointed Hebrew Old Testament would make God the author of confusion, which he is certainly not. *See* 1 Corinthians 14:33.

The issue was of utmost importance in the 17th and 18th centuries. The 17th century Helvetic (Swiss) Consensus Formula of 1675 noted the particular vowel points of the Hebrew Old Testament as being inspired by God.

> But, in particular, The Hebrew original of the OT which we have received and to this day do retain as handed down by the Hebrew Church, "who had been given the oracles of God" (Rom 3:2), is, **not only in its consonants, but in its vowels either the vowel points themselves, or at least the power of the points not only in its matter, but in its words, inspired by God.** It thus forms, together with the Original of the NT the sole and complete rule of our faith and practice; and to its

standard, as to a Lydian stone, all extant versions, eastern or western, ought to be applied, and wherever they differ, be conformed.[69]

In a video titled, *The Legacy Standard Bible Exposed*, the narrator explained:

> If the integrity of verbal plenary inspiration could be undermined by the denial of the originality of the Hebrew vowel points and the universalist view of Semitic religions could be granted and the obnoxious traditions of the Jews and their fables could be venerated then the stage was set for the stripping of the very name of God himself out of his people's mouths.[70]

He explained Satan's strategy to get people to forget God's true name and substitute the title of heathen god in his place. His strategy will fail because God examines the heart of his worshippers and understands that his sheep can be led astray. God states:

> **If we have forgotten the name of our God, or stretched out our hands to a strange god; Shall not God search this out? for he knoweth the secrets of the heart.** (Psalms 44:20-21 AV)

That does not mean that God's name is unimportant to him. Indeed, from his name flows great blessings.

> Because he hath set his love upon me, therefore will I deliver him: I will set him on high, **because he hath known my name. He shall call upon me, and I will answer him:** I will be with him in trouble; I will deliver him, and honour him. With long life will I satisfy him, and shew him my

salvation. (Psalms 91:14-16 AV)

It is for this reason that God is against the publishers of the modern Bibles who conceal his name from people and substitute heathen gods like Baal and Yahweh. The Bible publishers "steal' God's words from his Holy Bible.

> How long shall this be in the heart of the prophets that prophesy lies? yea, they are prophets of the deceit of their own heart; **Which think to cause my people to forget my name** by their dreams which they tell every man to his neighbour, **as their fathers have forgotten my name for Baal**. The prophet that hath a dream, let him tell a dream; and he that hath my word, **let him speak my word faithfully**. What is the chaff to the wheat? saith the LORD. Is not my word like as a fire? saith the LORD; and like a hammer that breaketh the rock in pieces? Therefore, behold, **I am against the prophets, saith the LORD, that steal my words** every one from his neighbour. Behold, **I am against the prophets, saith the LORD, that use their tongues, and say, He saith.** (Jeremiah 23:26-31 AV)

Sadly, the myth started by Elias Levita that the original Hebrew text was unpointed is the orthodox view today. Nowadays, the pointings in the Hebrew text are widely rejected as modern emendations made by the Masorites. Through that one myth, the apostate "Christians" have joined with the Jews and Catholics to remove the pesky vowels from the Hebrew Old Testament. The minions of Satan are now able to reconstruct YHVH and change it from Jehovah to Yahweh.

Dr. John Hinton, Ph.D., deconstructs the myth that the original Hebrew scriptures did not have vowel points.

First we must deal with the common myth and that is that there are no vowels expressed in the Hebrew text. This is a convenient line of nonsense for those who want to change the text to fit their own views, but it is a dishonest line. Elaborate diacritic marks, called pointing by English-speaking Hebrew scholars, provide extensive information for vowels, doubled letters, stops, and other phonological features. Bible "correctors" are either ignorant of this fact or they pretend that they do not exist. Those who are aware of them and argue that they may be ignored because they were introduced into the text by the Massoretes at a later date are giving themselves free rein to alter virtually every word in the entire Hebrew Old Testament. Not only do these biblical detractors deny God's promise to forever preserve his word, every jot and tittle, but they open the door for Bible manipulation that has no other criteria than personal judgment or fancy. If we are to deny the Masoretic reading we can do no end of mischief to the text by inserting our own vowels, doubled letters, and stops. This allows us to change positives into negatives, passives into actives and vice versa, statement verbs into causative verbs and vice versa, to convert verbs into nouns and vice versa, and to even change the entire meaning of the verb itself. Many words could have several or even a dozen different varied meanings by toying with the pointing. Furthermore, some diacritics indicate different letters entirely. A dot over the right side of a shin indicates an SH, while a dot over the left side of it indicates an S. A dot inside of a *vav* is pronounce like a long U while a dot over the *vav* turns it into an O, so the removal or addition of such a dot is fair game to the Yahweh crowd. A dot inside a Pe is pronounced like P, while if it lacks a dot it become an F. Similarly a Bet with a dot is a B and a V without one. A number of other letters have similar features of changing their sounds according to the presence or position of a dot. If we are to ignore the vowel pointings, we are equally justified in changing S to SH and vice versa, or many other consonant changes, since the Massoretes were responsible for the consonant identifying diacritics as well. Suggestions to alter the text is a common method of attacking the Bible that has been employed by Bible-scoffing scholars in academia for over 100 years, it is a common practice that I encountered frequently among fellow students in Hebrew classes. The practice is taught and encouraged by those who consider the Bible to be mythology.

It is amazing to see this being done by people who claim to honor the Bible. Dr. G.A. Riplinger, in her tome, [*In Awe of Thy Word*], points out that ignoring the vowel marks in the Hebrew allow Jews and atheists to remove future references to our Saviour from the Old Testament by toying with these vowels. [Riplinger, pp. 433-434]. For this reason vowelless Tanakhs (Hebrew name for Old Testament) are sometimes used. In fact, if the Masoretic diacritics are ignored, there is scarcely a word in the entire Bible, if there is any at all, that cannot be altered or changed completely. Why is it that alleged Bible-believers think that it is wrong to change words in the Bible into entirely different words, but it is alright to ignore the reading of the Hebrew text and alter the name of God without any evidence to support their altered reading other than the opinion of 19th century atheists? In fact, they are changing it when linguistic evidence shows that the pronunciation that they are using is wrong.[71]

The vowel points for YHVH prove that the Hebrew YHVH cannot be translated into Yahweh. Yahweh is missing a vowel. There are three vowel points. Yahweh only has two vowels. *Vav* (ו) can only be pronounced as a hard "v" sound in this context. Yahweh

יְהֹוָה

JEHOVAH

argues for a soft "w" sound. The soft "w" sound is an Arabic pronunciation of *vav* (ו); it is not Hebrew.[72] The soft vowel sound required for Yahweh makes no sense; since, in this context, the *vav* (ו) would be preceded by the vowel point *holem* having a long "o" sound and followed by another vowel point *kamatz* with a short "a" sound. That would be three vowel sounds in a row. If we stick with the three vowel points and go with the soft consonants preferred by the Yahweh camp, the actual pronunciation for Yahweh ends up being Yahowah (Y-eh-h-oh-ow-ah-h). That sounds nothing like Yahweh. The proper construction should be Jehovah (J-eh-h-oh-v-ah-h). Finally, the correct English translation for *yod* (י) require a hard "J" sound. Indeed, all the Hebrew words starting with *yod* (י) like Joseph, Jerusalem, Jericho, etc. are translated with a hard "J" sound in English. *See* Psalms 119:73 in the KJV where *yod* (י) is rendered *jod* in English. But Yahweh needs a soft "Y" sound.

The vowel points in the original Hebrew Old Testament scriptures impeach the claim that the Tetragrammaton YHVH is Yahweh. The clear evidence establishes that the AV translation of Jehovah is correct. Dr. John Hinton explains how the duped "Christians" are being led astray by ignorantly following the superstitious beliefs of heathen scholars and their god, Yahweh.

What is amusing is that those who make a big deal

47

out of the conversion to J, and who contradict the Bible by calling God Yahweh while still calling themselves Bible-believers generally know about as much about Hebrew as the average Australian aborigine knows about Lithuanian. It troubles me how very few people realize that the god that they now worship, named Yahweh, is derived from a storm god created by atheist scholars following in the steps of the late 19th century skeptics, and that these atheists are feeding them much of their theology.[73]

# 6 Theophoric Names Prove God's Name is Jehovah

God has locked in Jehovah as his name in his inspired Old Testament. In Psalms 68:4 we find that God identifies himself as **JAH**, a contraction of *JEHOVAH*.

> Sing unto God, sing praises to his name: extol him that rideth upon the heavens by his name **JAH**, and rejoice before him. (Psalms 68:4 AV)

In Exodus 15:2, the AV translators translated **JAH** as LORD.

> **The LORD [JAH]** is my strength and song, and he is become my salvation: he is my God, and I will prepare him an habitation; my father's God, and I will exalt him. **The LORD [JEHOVAH]** is a man of war: **the LORD [JEHOVAH]** is his name." (Exodus 15:2-3 AV)

**JAH** (יָהּ) is a contraction of *JEHOVAH*. The AV translators correctly rendered JAH as LORD in the AV. Indeed at

49

Exodus 15:2. Jehovah was commonly translated as the LORD with all capital letters in the AV. For example, in the very next verse, after we find the AV translators rendered JAH as the LORD in Exodus 15:2, the AV translators translated Jehovah as the LORD in Exodus 15:3. The translators understood that **JAH** was a contraction of *JEHOV***AH**.

יָהּ

JAH

God himself said his name is JAH in Psalms 68:4; he also said his hame is JEHOVAH in Exodus 6:3. Thus equating the two names, and confirming that JAH is a contraction of JEHOVAH. Indeed, God states in Psalms 83:10 "That men may know that thou, **whose name alone is JEHOVAH**, art the most high over all the earth."

A theophoric name embeds the name of God in a person's name and indicates something about God or a person's relationship with God. God has locked in his name as Jehovah by using of two sets of theophoric names.[74] JAH is seen as part of the theophoric names in the Bible.[75] JAH = IAH as a suffix in theophoric namcs. Below are some examples.

Amaz**iah** (1 Kings 12:21) means Jehovah is mighty.
Athal**iah** (2 Kings 11:3) means afflicted of Jehovah.
Hezek**iah** (2 Kings 18:1) means Jehovah is my strength.
Jedid**iah** (2 Samuel 12:25) means beloved of Jehovah.
Jerem**iah** (Jeremiah 27:1) means Jehovah has founded.
Jos**iah** (1 Kings 13:2), means whom Jehovah heals.
Obad**iah** (1 Chronicles 3:21) means servant of

Jehovah.

Uriah (2 Samuel 11:3), means Jehovah is my light.

Zachariah (2 Kings 14:29) means Jehovah remembers.

Zedekiah (1 Kings 22:11) means Jehovah is righteous.

The Yahweh worshipers claim that JAH is not a contraction of Jehovah but rather an abbreviation of Yahweh that should be rendered YAH. Indeed, the LSB changes JAH to YAH in Psalms 68:4, with a footnote claiming that YAH is a "shortened form of Yahweh." There is a problem with that argument. The theophoric name Elijah is a fly in their ointment. Eli**jah** means my God is **JAH (JEHOVAH)**. The LSB translators did not change Elijah's name. The LSB repeatedly refers to him as Elijah, not Eliyah, as their allegiance to Yahweh requires. *See, e.g.,* 1 Kings 18 LSB. Indeed, all English Bible Versions, including the Hebraic Roots Bible, render the Hebrew as Elijah in English.

The theophoric name Eli**jah** stands as testimony that God's name in English is **JAH**, which is a contraction of **JEHOVAH**. The very text of the LSB containing Eli**jah**'s name impeaches the LSB claim that the LORD's name is Yahweh.

Another problem with the Yahweh worshipers' argument is that there is another set of theophoric names based on an abreviation of God's name. Those theophoric words make Yahweh an impossibility. Those thosphoric names start with **JEHO**, which is an abbreviation of **JEHO***VAH*. **JEHO** uses the first two consonants of **JEHO***VAH* to form the prefix in theophoric names. Below are some examples.

**Jeho**adah (1 Chronicles 8:36) means Jehovah has adorned.

**Jeho**addan (2 Chronicles 25:1) means Jehovah delights.

**Jeho**ahaz (2 Kings 10:35) means Jehovah has grasped.

**Jeho**ash (2 Kings 11:21) means Jehovah is strong.

**Jeho**hanan (1 Chronicles 26:3) means Jehovah has been gracious.

**Jeho**iachin (2 Kings 24:6) means Jehovah appoints.

**Jeho**iada (2 Samual 8:18) means Jehovah knows.

**Jeho**iakim (2 Kings 23:34) means Jehovah raises up.

**Jeho**iarib (1 Chronicles 9:10) means Jehovah contends..

**Jeho**nadab (2 Kings 10:15) means Jehovah is noble.

Notice that JEHO has two syllables. That fact excludes Yahweh as the root because Yahweh has two syllables in total, and the vowel sounds are not the same. JEHO has a short "e" sound followed by a long "o" sound. There is no long "o" sound in Yahweh. Yahweh has a short "a" sound followed by a short "e" sound. The vowels in the theophoric names beginning with JEHO do not match the vowel sounds in Yahweh. God is revealing through the theophoric names that his name in English can only be Jehovah; it is impossible that God's name is Yahweh.

(There is No "O" in Yahweh)

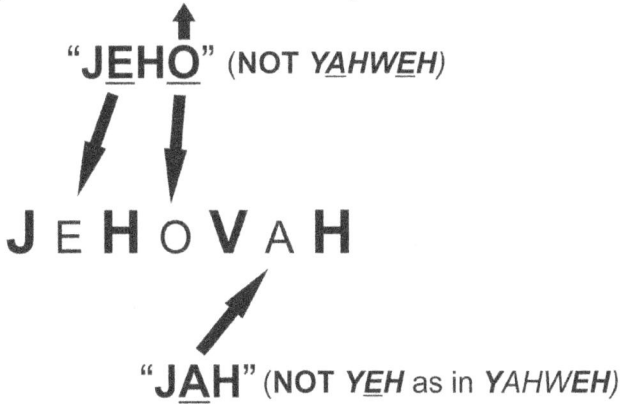

## "JEHO" (NOT Y<u>A</u>HW<u>E</u>H)

## J E H O V A H

## "J<u>A</u>H" (NOT Y<u>E</u>H as in YAHWEH)

# Elijah means my God is JAH (JEHOVAH)

**JAH** is a contraction of **JEHOVAH**. See Psalms 68:4. It is used in the suffix of theophoric names in the Bible in the form of IAH, as in Jos**iah**. **JEHO** is an abbreviation of **JEHOVAH**. It is used in the prefix of theophoric names such as **Jeho**adah. The "o" poses a serious problem for the Yahweh promoters. There is no "o" in Yahweh. There is no way to fit Yahweh into both sets of theophoric names. The vowels must be as in Jehovah and cannot be as in Yahweh. God has locked in his divine name as Jehovah in English by these two sets of theophoric names. Confirmation that God's name in English is Jehovah is found in the theophoric name Elijah. Eli**jah** means my God (אל) is **JAH** (יה) (JEHOVAH). The theophoric name Elijah makes Yahweh an impossibility. All English Bible versions, including the LSB and the Hebraic Roots Bible, render the Hebrew אליה as Eli**jah** in English. The theophoric name Elijah impeaches rendering the Tetragrammaton (YHVH) as Yahweh in the modern English Bible versions.

53

# 7 Jesus Christ Is Jehovah

D r. Nehemia Gordon, Ph.D., is a Hebraist who explains that Jehovah literally means He who was, He who is, and He who will be.[76] He states in Genesis 3:14 where God said: "I AM THAT I AM," *Ehyah asher Ehyah* reveals what God meant by Jehovah in Genesis 3:15 (translated as "the LORD" in the AV). Dr. Jordan states that "I AM" in Genesis 3:14 explains "the LORD" (Jehovah) in Genesis 3:15. He describes how Jehovah is three forms of the Hebrew verb "to be." *Hayah* (He was) *Hoveh* (He who is), and *Yihyeh* (He will be).

היה הוה יהיה

Hayah     Hoveh     Yihyeh

He Who Was    He Who Is    He Who Will Be

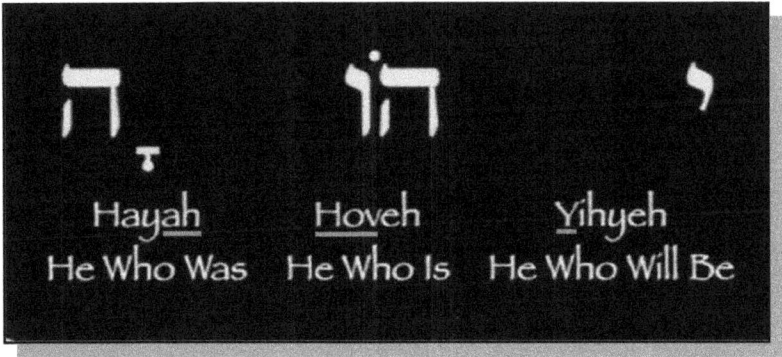

ה<sub>ָ</sub>ה ‏הֹ‏וּ‏ ‏י‏

Hayah        Hoveh        Yihyeh
He Who Was   He Who Is    He Who Will Be

‏יְהֹ‏וָ‏ה‏

(Hebrew-Right to Left)
**JEHOVAH**
(English-Left to Right)

Dr. Gordon is a Karaite Jew. Karaite Jews only recognize the Tanakh (a.k.a., Old Testament) as authoritative in Jewish religious law and theology. In contrast to mainstream Rabbinic Judaism, Karaite Jews eschew other sources like the Talmud and Kabbalah as being authoritative. As a Jew, Dr. Gordon does not believe that Jesus is Christ. Nonetheless, he honestly explains that the same meaning for God's name in Jehovah is found in the book of Revelation, where it says that the Lord is he "which art, and wast, and shalt be" (i.e., the Lord is Jehovah). That confirms that the proper meaning in Revelation 16:5 is as in the AV: "And I heard the angel of the waters say, Thou art righteous, O Lord, **which art, and wast, and shalt be**, because thou hast judged thus." (Revelation 16:5 AV) And we see in Revelations 1:8, Jesus is Jehovah. "I am Alpha and Omega, the beginning and the ending, saith the Lord, **which is, and which was, and which is to come,**

55

the Almighty." (Revelation 1:8 AV)

Nick Sayers explains how the reference to Jesus as Lord means he is Jehovah.

> The authors of the New Testament under inspiration from God translated the Hebrew Jehovah (*Yehovah*) as the Greek *Kurios*, which means "Lord" That is why the KJV translators translated Jehovah as LORD in the Old Testament. One important feature when learning translation methodology is examining how words are carried across (translated) from the Old Testament into the New Testament by the original writers. The King James Version translators knew that if God translated the Hebrew Jehovah (*Yehovah*) as the Greek *Kurios* without any issues, then such methods were also safe to replicate into the English tongue.[77]

God explains this in Philippians 2:11:

> Wherefore God also hath highly exalted him, and given him **a name which is above every name**: That at the name of Jesus every knee should bow, of things in heaven, and things in earth, and things under the earth; And that every tongue should confess that Jesus Christ is **Lord**, to the glory of God the Father. Philippians 2:11.

The modern Bible versions undermine the deity of Jesus Christ. For example, in Luke 23:42, the thief on the cross, being born again by God and given the gift of faith, turned to Jesus and called him Lord. The new Bible versions remove the word Lord and have the thief addressing Jesus without indicating that he was recognizing and addressing the Lord God Almighty on the cross.

|            AV            |            ESV            |
|--------------------------|---------------------------|
| And he said unto Jesus, **Lord**, remember me when thou comest into thy kingdom. (Luke 23:42 AV) | And he said, **"Jesus**, remember me when you come into your kingdom." (Luke 23:42 ESV) |

These textual alterations began with the 1885 Revised Version (RV) of the Bible, spearheaded by Brooke Foss Westcott and Fenton John Anthony Hort. The corruptions have been incorporated into most of the modern Bible versions. Westcott tried to justify the many alterations of the Holy Bible while working on the committee of the Revised Version of the Bible. In his book, *Some Lessons of the Revised Version of the New Testament*, Westcott alleged that the removed references to the deity of Jesus Christ were not removals at all. He claimed that the inclusion of "Lord" and "Christ" in Jesus' name in the Textus Receptus (Received Text) was simply due to "inattentive scribes." His mission was to accentuate the humanity of Jesus. Thus, the titles "Lord" and "Christ" needed to go. That resulted in a diminution of his deity in the RV.

> The emphasis which is here laid on the human name Jesus, which fixes attention on the fact of the true humanity of the Lord, is implied in many other passages where the inattention of scribes has led to the alteration of the simple name. For example, we read — I John i. 7: the blood of Jesus (Authorised Version, Jesus Christ) his Son cleanseth us from all sin. I John iv. 3: every spirit which confesseth not Jesus (Authorised Version, Jesus Christ; comp. marg.). Heb. iii. i: consider the Apostle and High Priest of our confession, even Jesus (Authorised Version, Christ Jesus). Luke xxiii. 42: he said, Jesus (Authorised Version, said unto Jesus, Lord) remember me when thou comest in thy kingdom.

Acts xvi. 31: believe on the Lord Jesus (Authorised Version adds Christ). Acts xix. 4: that they should believe on him which should come after him, that is, on Jesus (Authorised Version, Christ Jesus).[78]

This diminishment of the deity of the Lord Jesus Christ was done as part of a plot wherein slight changes would be made to the text in the Revised Version, the significance of which would go unnoticed. The Revised Version was intended to alter articles of faith through the cumulative effect of the seemingly inconsequential changes. The doctrinal changes would only be discerned when compiled and read together. Westcott explained the strategy in the 1897 book he wrote about his work on the New Testament Committee of the 1885 Revised Version of the Bible.

But the value of the Revision is most clearly seen when the student considers together a considerable group of passages, which **bear upon some article of the Faith.** The accumulation of small details then produces its full effect. Points on which it might have seemed pedantic to insist in a single passage become impressive by repetition.[79]

Westcott knew that the cumulative effect of changes he was making in the Revised Version would change the articles of the Christian faith. That was the objective. Westcott's cohort in this spiritual crime was Fenton John Anthony Hort. Hort explained how what would appear to be negligible changes, a little here and a little there, cumulatively would significantly impact Christian doctrine. He analogized their work on the Revised Version of the Bible to a forger of paintings who makes the painting so close to the original that the forgery goes unnoticed.

The forgery of an artwork is an apt analogy to what they were doing. They were creating a forgery, a false Bible that was intended to make doctrinal changes and create a falsified new brand of "Christianity." Hort explained in a July 19, 1870, letter to an unknown friend the concept behind the changes in the Revised Version while he was beginning his work along with Wescott on the committee of the Revised Version of the Bible.

> Our work of last week gave even better promise than the former session. The spirit was almost incredibly good. ... **It is quite impossible to judge of the value of what appear to be trifling alterations merely by reading them one after another. Taken together, they have often important bearings which few would think of at first.** There is but one safe rule, to be as scrupulously exact as possible, remembering, of course, that there is a truth of tone as well as of grammar and dictionary. The difference between a picture say of Raffaelle and a feeble copy of it is made up of a number of trivial differences.[80]

Seventeen years before beginning work on the committee for the Revised Version of the Bible, Hort was scheming with Westcott to use the corrupt Alexandrian Greek texts to supplant the Majority Byzantine Greek texts that were the basis for the KJV. In his mind, he considered the genuine Byzantine Greek texts to be "corrupt." He was working with the con man Constantin von Tishendorf (1815-1874), who foisted the corrupted Greek Codex Sinaiticus upon the world. Hort and Westcott would use the Codex Sinaiticus to do much mischief in their Revised Version of the Bible, which was later published in 1885. In 1853, Hort wrote the following to John Ellerton.

> He [Wescott] and I are going to edit a Greek text of the N. T. some two or three years hence, if possible. Lachmann and Tischendorf will supply rich materials, but not nearly enough; and we hope to do a good deal with the Oriental versions. **Our**

**object is to supply clergymen generally, schools, etc., with a portable Gk. Test., which shall not be disfigured with Byzantine corruptions.**[81]

Their strategy was first to get their corrupted Bible into seminaries and pulpits to then change the Christian articles of faith into something very different from what is portrayed in the Holy Scriptures as given in the King James Holy Bible.

Despite the express words of the principal conspirators, Westcott and Hort, that they were engaged in a plot to change the Christian doctrine, advocates of the new Bible versions claim that there is no such plot. Mike Leake gives the common argument dismissing concerns over the new Bible versions.

There is no plot to undermine the word of God. These are very conservative scholars that are doing the work of textual criticism to help us have the most accurate translation of the Bible as possible. And lest anyone think, with all this talk of textual variants, that your Bible cannot be trusted heed these words of David Alan Black:

"No biblical doctrine would go unsupported if a favorite reading was abandoned in favor of a more valid variant…a doctrine that is affected by textual variation will always be adequately supported by other passages."[82]

Leake and Black miss the point. The strategy of Westcott and Hort was to make small changes so that the changes would be less noticeable but which, in the aggregate, would change doctrine. Leake's and David Alan Black's argument that no doctrine is undermined by a textual change in the new Bible versions is countered well by James H. Son.[83] His statement was mentioned earlier in this book but is worth repeating. James Son states the

60

logic of the new Bible version defenders is like arguing that there is no harm in removing a stop sign from a busy street intersection because the other traffic signals in the city were left intact. Even though the sign only contained one word, that word is critically important to those who arrive at the intersection. So also is each word in the Holy Bible of critical importance to those reading it. God has made the point in the Holy Bible that **every word of God** is essential, not just some of the words. "[M]an shall not live by bread alone, but by **every word of God**." (Luke 4:4 AV) Disturbingly but unsurprisingly, the last clause, "but by **every word of God**," was deleted from the RV and almost all new Bible versions.

Deleting that clause from Luke 4:4 strips the passage of all spiritual guidance and enlightenment. Jesus's point was that man is given life by his word, but the new Bible versions remove that truth and instead are left only to learn that man needs more than bread to live, like water and meat. It is a different doctrine. It changes a truth about spiritual health into advice about physical health. It changes an article of faith, just as Westcott and Hort said their changes would do.

It seems that Hort accepted the Arian heresy that Jesus Christ was not the eternal God but rather was created by God. Under the Arian theology, Jesus did not always exist and, therefore, is not coeternal with God the Father. We see evidence of Hort's Arianism in his commentary on Revelation 3:14. That Bible passage states: "And unto the angel of the church of the Laodiceans write; These things saith the Amen, the faithful and true witness, the beginning of the creation of God." (Revelation 3:14 AV)

Hort interpreted the statement that the faithful witness, the Amen, Jesus Christ, being the beginning of the creation of God in Revelation 3:14 meant that God created Jesus. Hort states: **"The words might no doubt bear the Arian meaning 'the first thing**

61

**created.'"**[84] Hort also held out the possibility that Jesus Christ was "antecedent" to all creation and cited Colossians 1:16 and 1:18 for that possibility. But, oddly, Hort used the word "antecedent" to creation. Antecedent simply means to come before something. It is not the same thing as existing in eternity before creation. There is a difference. The gospel is that Jesus is the eternal God and creator of all things. See Colossians 1:16-18. Jesus did not simply come before creation; he is the eternal creator of all things. But Hort puts Jesus only "antecedent" to creation.

Hort suggests that Jesus was not God, the creator, but simply a vehicle through "whom all creation came and comes to pass." Hort has Jesus being something less than fully God. Hort seemed to lean toward the view that the passage in Revelation 3:14 "might no doubt" mean that Jesus was created by God the Father and is, thus, not the eternal Lord God Almighty presented in the inspired scriptures.

The Arian heresy is premised on the misinterpretation of what scripture means when it says that Jesus Christ is "the only begotten Son of God." See John 3:18. Arius, the namesake for Arianism, called God the Father, unbegotten, but Jesus Christ is God's begotten Son.[85] Arius said that the Son was begotten before the world was created. But because he emanated from God the Father, he is not eternal nor coeternal with God the Father.[86]

What Arius got wrong is that he did not understand the point at which Jesus Christ was begotten. Jesus was begotten by God at his resurrection in fulfilment of the prophecy in Psalm 2:7.

> But God raised him from the dead: And he was seen many days of them which came up with him from Galilee to Jerusalem, who are his witnesses unto the people. And we declare unto you glad tidings, how that the promise which was made unto the fathers, **God hath fulfilled the same unto us**

**their children, in that he hath raised up Jesus
again**; as it is also written in the second psalm,
Thou art my Son, **this day have I begotten thee**.
(Acts 13:30-33 KJV)

The importance of that truth is that believers will, in like
manner, be resurrected to eternal life as adopted sons of God.

For if we have been planted together in the
likeness of his death, we shall be also in the
likeness of his resurrection:" (Romans 6:5 KJV)

The changes made by Westcott and Hort that undermine
the eternal character of Jesus Christ are doctrinal. They go to the
heart of the gospel. The Lord Jesus Christ is God. Jesus Christ and
the Father are one. John 10:30. "For there is one God, and one
mediator between God and men, the man Christ Jesus." 1 Timothy
2:5. Indeed, when Jesus was on Earth, he was in heaven
simultaneously. "And no man hath ascended up to heaven, but he
that came down from heaven, **even the Son of man which is in
heaven**." (John 3:13 AV) God the Father is in heaven. Matthew
23:9. That verse testifies to Jesus Christ being the imnipresent God
Almighty. But the Arians could not allow that pasage to remain,
and so they removed it from the Greek text. Consequently, the
modern Bible versions contain John 3:13 without any indication
of the omnipresence of Jesus Christ.

| AV | NIV |
|---|---|
| And no man hath ascended up to heaven, but he that came down from heaven, even the Son of man **which is in heaven.** (John 3:13 AV) | No one has ever gone into heaven except the one who came from heaven—the Son of Man. (John 3:13 NIV) |

Brooke Foss Westcott's claim that he changed Bible

passages (e.g., Luke 23:42) to emphasize Jesus Christ's humanity is a cover for his true motive to undermine the deity of Jesus Christ in accordance with the Arian heresy. Jesus Christ is the eternal God Almighty who came to Earth in the flesh. The gospel of Mark reveals that Jesus is Jehovah, the LORD of hosts. Mark 1:1-3 states:

> The beginning of the gospel of Jesus Christ, the Son of God; As it is written in the prophets, Behold, I send my messenger before thy face, which shall prepare thy way before **thee**. The voice of one crying in the wilderness, Prepare ye the way of **the Lord**, make his paths straight. (Mark 1:1-3 AV)

That passage contains two quotes from two different prophets, Malachi and Isaiah. The first quote is from Malachi 3:1. That passage in Malachi states:

> Behold, I will send my messenger, and he shall prepare the way before **me**: and the Lord, whom ye seek, shall suddenly come to his temple, even the messenger of the covenant, whom ye delight in: behold, he shall come, saith **the LORD of hosts**. (Malachi 3:1 AV)

Notice that Jehovah is speaking in Malachi, and he is prophesying his coming. Jehovah, in Malachi 3:1, prophesies about the messenger that would go before him. The LORD of hosts states that his messenger will prepare the way for him. We learn in Mark 1 that the prophesied messenger referenced in Malachi 3:1 is John the Baptist, who God said would go before "**me**," meaning the LORD of hosts. The word LORD in English is

64

a translation of the Hebrew (Jehovah) in Malachi 3:1. But when the passage is quoted in Mark 1:1-3, the inspired word of God states that the messenger would go before "**thee**," which is second person singular objective pronoun; it is referring to Jesus Christ. But Malachi 3:1 uses the word "**me**," which is also a singular objective pronoun, but it relates to the speaker in first person, who is Jehovah, "the LORD of hosts." Thus, we see that Jesus is Jehovah.

This is confirmed by the passage in Mark 1:1-3 that follows the quote from Malachi 3:1 with a quote from Isaiah 40:3. The Isaiah prophesy is that the crier in the wilderness calls on the people to prepare the way of the LORD. The word LORD in Isaiah 40:3 is, once again, a Hebrew word (Jehovah), translated as LORD in English. But we know that the prophecy in Isaiah 40:3 is being fulfilled by John the Baptist and refers to him preparing the way for the Lord Jesus Christ.

The voice of him that crieth in the wilderness,
Prepare ye the way of the LORD, make straight in
the desert a highway for our God. (Isaiah 40:3 AV)

Thus, the passage in Mark 1:1-3 establishes that the Lord for whom the way was to be made straight is the same LORD prophesied in Isaiah 40:3. That LORD in Isaiah 40:3 is Jehovah, which means that the Lord in Mark 1:1-3 is also Jehovah. Mark 1:1-3 describes the coming of the Lord Jesus Christ. Thus, Jesus Christ is Jehovah, the LORD of hosts, who came in the flesh.

When Jesus said in John 14:9, "he that hath seen me hath seen the Father," he meant that literally. Jesus explained in no uncertain terms that "I and my Father are one." John 10:30. Jesus identified himself as God almighty. God told Moses he is the eternal "I AM." Exodus 3:14. Jesus also identified himself as the eternal "I AM." "Jesus said unto them, Verily, verily, I say unto you, Before Abraham was, **I am**." John 8:58.

Jesus and Jehovah are one. That is because if Jehovah is God and Jesus is God, then they must necessarily be one. "And the LORD shall be king over all the earth: in that day shall there be one LORD, and his name **one**." (Zechariah 14:9 AV) We read in 1 John 5:7 that "there are three that bear record in heaven, the Father, the Word, and the Holy Ghost: and these three are **one**." In Deuteronomy, we learn that God is one. "Hear, O Israel: **The LORD our God is one LORD**: And thou shalt love the LORD thy God with all thine heart, and with all thy soul, and with all thy might." (Deuteronomy 6:4-5 AV) Jesus reinforced that truth by quoting the Deuteronomy passage in Mark:

> And one of the scribes came, and having heard them reasoning together, and perceiving that he had answered them well, asked him, Which is the first commandment of all? And Jesus answered him, The first of all the commandments is, Hear, O Israel; **The Lord our God is one Lord**: And thou shalt love the Lord thy God with all thy heart, and with all thy soul, and with all thy mind, and with all thy strength: this is the first commandment. (Mark 12:28-30 AV)

JEHOVAH is God; that is his name (Exodus 6:3, Pslams 83:18); he is our salvation. "Behold, God is my salvation; I will trust, and not be afraid: for the LORD JEHOVAH is my strength and my song; he also is become my salvation." (Isaiah 12:2 AV) We read in Luke how Jesus was born Christ the Lord to save his elect from their sins. "For unto you is born this day in the city of David a Saviour, which is Christ the Lord." (Luke 2:11 AV) It was necessary that God save us from our sins because, as God explains, only he can be our savior. "I, even I, am the LORD; and beside me there is no saviour." Isaiah 43:11. The word LORD in Isaiah 43:11 is a Hebrew word (Jehovah), translated as LORD in English. That means that only Jehovah can be the savior; there can be no other. Thus, Jesus Christ must necessarily be Jehovah.

Indeed, God the Father makes it clear that his Son, Jesus, our savior, is God. "But unto the **Son** he saith, Thy throne, **O God**, is for ever and ever: a sceptre of righteousness *is* the sceptre of thy kingdom." (Hebrews 1:8) The birth of Jesus Christ fulfilled the prophecies in Isaiah 9:6 and Micah 5:2, explaining that the everlasting Lord God Almighty would be the savior born in Bethlehem. God was born as a child to save his elect from their sins. Matthew 1:21. That child was Jesus Christ, God manifest in the flesh. *See* 1 Timothy 3:16. God the Father gets the glory when every knee should bow and every tongue should confess that Jesus Christ is Lord because Jesus Christ and God the Father are one Lord.

> That at the name of Jesus every knee should bow, of things in heaven, and things in earth, and things under the earth; And that every tongue should confess that Jesus Christ is Lord, to the glory of God the Father. (Philippians 2:10-11 AV)

God is one Lord. Deuteronomy 6:4-5. That means that the child savior born at Bethlehem was the one Lord God Almighty. Jesus Christ is one with the Godhead. *See* 1 John 5:7-8. "For in him dwelleth all the fulness of the Godhead bodily." (Colossians 2:9 AV). That is how Jesus Christ was both on Earth and in heaven simultaneously. *See* John 3:13. Thus, Christ (The Prince of Peace, John 14:27), the Holy Spirit (Wonderful Counsellor, John 14:16-18), and God the Father (the everlasting Father, John 14:9-10) all dwell in Jesus Christ because God is one Lord.

> For unto us a child is born, unto us a son is given: and the government shall be upon his shoulder: **and his name shall be called Wonderful, Counsellor, The mighty God, The everlasting Father, The Prince of Peace.** (Isaiah 9:6 AV)

God left heaven and came to Earth as a man to give

himself as a sacrifice to atone for our sins so that his elect could inherit eternal life. That is the heart of the gospel. "Who was delivered for our offences, and was raised again for our justification." Romans 4:25. As Paul said to Timothy:

> And without controversy great is the mystery of godliness: **God was manifest in the flesh**, justified in the Spirit, seen of angels, preached unto the Gentiles, believed on in the world, received up into glory. 1 Timothy 3:16.

Defenders of the modern Bible versions claim that the essential doctrines of the Christian faith are expressed in the new Bible versions, even though they have been deleted in a particular passage. Dr. James White, for example, claims that no textual variant in any modern Bible version in any way, shape, or form materially disrupts or destroys any essential doctrine of the Christian faith.[87] The promoters of the modern Bibles claim a deleted doctrine in the new Bibles can still be found in other Bible passages. That is not true. And John 3:13 reveals the lie. John 3:13 is the only passage in the Holy Bible that explains the omnipresence of Jesus Christ. Deleting that truth, as do the modern Bible versions, deletes that truth from the gospel.

If Jesus is not God then we have no savior. The Holy Bible tells us that only the Lord God can be our savior. **"I, even I, am the LORD; and beside me there is no saviour."** Isaiah 43:11. The new Bible versions that undermine the deity of Jesus Christ undermine the gospel of salvation by his atoning blood through God's grace by the faith of Jesus Christ. Only the Lord can be our savior. If Jesus is not the Lord, we have no savior.

We find the Arian philosophy in subtle ways in the new Bible versions that spring from the Westcott and Hort Greek text. We read in Micah 5:2 about the prophecy of Christ, the eternal God, being born in Bethlehem. Christ is described as being "from everlasting." The definition of everlasting is: "Eternity; eternal duration, past and future. From everlasting to everlasting thou art God. Psalms 90:2."[88] Everlasting means having no beginning and no end.

But the passage in Micah 5:2 that describes Christ in the new Bible versions changes the description of Christ being "from everlasting" to being only "from ancient times." The new Bible versions support the Arian heresy. This is a subtle change, but it is a proof text that identifies Jesus Christ as the eternal Lord God Almighty, born in Bethelem. The new Bible versions render Jesus Christ as only being around a long time, implying that he had a beginning and thus is not the eternal God.

| AV | NIV |
|---|---|
| But thou, Bethlehem Ephratah, though thou be little among the thousands of Judah, yet out of thee shall he come forth unto me that is to be ruler in Israel; **whose goings forth have been from of old, from everlasting**. (Micah 5:2 AV) | But you, Bethlehem Ephrathah, though you are small among the clans of Judah, out of you will come for me one who will be ruler over Israel, **whose origins are from of old, from ancient times**. (Micah 5:2 NIV) |

Another example of the removal of language that identifies Jesus Christ as the eternal God Almighty is found in the modern Bible versions of Revelation 1:11. Jesus Christ identifies himself as "Alpha and Omega, the first and the last." But the modern Bibles founded on Westcott and Hort's work remove that truth.

| AV | NLT |
|---|---|
| I was in the Spirit on the Lord's day, and heard behind me a great voice, as of a trumpet, Saying, **I am Alpha and Omega, the first and the last**: and, What thou seest, write in a book, and send it unto the seven churches which are in Asia; unto Ephesus, and unto Smyrna, and unto Pergamos, and unto Thyatira, and unto Sardis, and unto Philadelphia, and unto Laodicea. (Revelation 1:10-11 AV) | It was the Lord's Day, and I was worshiping in the Spirit. Suddenly, I heard behind me a loud voice like a trumpet blast. It said, "Write in a book everything you see, and send it to the seven churches in the cities of Ephesus, Smyrna, Pergamum, Thyatira, Sardis, Philadelphia, and Laodicea." (Revelation 1:10-11 NLT) |

There is a reason that the identification of Jesus as the Alpha and Omega is missing from Revelation 1:11. That is because Hort considered the reference to the Alpha and Omega in the preceding passages at John 1:4 and 1:8 to be a reference to God the Father to the exclusion of Jesus Christ.

Hort's view that Alpha and Omega in Revelation 1:4 and 1:8 could not reference Jesus Christ proves that Hort did not believe that Jesus Christ is God Almighty. The statement that "I am Alpha and Omega, the beginning and the ending, saith the Lord, which is, and which was, and which is to come, the Almighty" in Revelation 1:8 identifies Jesus Christ as Jehovah. Jesus Christ and God the Father are one.

But Hort does not believe in the deity of Jesus Christ as revealed in the gospel.[89] And so he analyzes Revelation 1:8 to preclude it from referring to Jesus Christ. That means the clear reference to the Alpha and Omega in Revelation 1:11 had to go. That dirty work was done by the Alexandrian Greek text forgers, which Westcott and Hort pressed into action. And so the Revised Version New Testament committee, under the influence of Westcott and Hort, followed the corrupt Alexandrian text and deleted the reference to Alpha and Omega in Revelation 1:11. In the following quote, please note that Hort is analyzing the Greek from the corrupt Alexandrian text of Revelation 1:8. Hort stated:

> This verse [Revelation 1:8] must stand alone. The speaker cannot be our Lord, when we consider Apoc. 1:4, which makes *oJ wJn* & c. distinctive of the Father; and all Scriptural analogy is against the attribution of *Kuvrio" oJ qeov"* [Lord God] with or without *pantokravtwr*, [the Almighty] G4120, to Christ. The verse is thus the utterance of the great fundamental voice of the Supreme God, preceding all separate revelations concerning or through His Son.[90]

Hort is revealing why the modern translations use the title "Lord God" instead of "Lord" in Revelation 1:8. It is a contrivance based on a corrupt theology that "Lord God" can only refer to God the Father to the exclusion of the Lord Jesus Christ. But when read in context, it is clear that Revelation 1:4 and Revelation 1:8 reference the Lord Jesus Christ. But the insertion of "Lord God" in Revelation 1:8 reveals Westcott and Hort's agenda is to undermine the deity of Jesus Christ by claiming that the Alpha and Omega is a reference to God the Father only and not at all to the Lord Jesus Christ.

This seemingly innocuous change from "Lord" to "Lord God" in Revelations 1:8 would go unnoticed as a doctrinal change when seen in isolation. But the stratagem becomes apparent when combined with the deletion of 1 John 5:7, Alpha and Omega in

Revelation 1:11, and the many other changes. Hort let the cat out of the bag when he explained his erroneous view that Alpha and Omega in Revelation 1:4 and 1:8 do not refer to the Lord Jesus Christ. Thus, the change in Revelation 1:8 from "Lord" to "Lord God" is given new meaning. It is part of the scheme. All of these small changes have a purpose. They are being done to obscure the deity of the Lord Jesus Christ.

| AV | RV |
|---|---|
| Behold, he cometh with clouds; and every eye shall see him, and **they also which pierced him**: and all kindreds of the earth shall wail because of him. Even so, Amen. I am Alpha and Omega, the beginning and the ending, saith **the Lord**, which is, and which was, and which is to come, the Almighty. (Revelation 1:7-8 AV) | Behold, he cometh with the clouds; and every eye shall see him, and **they which pierced him**; and all the tribes of the earth shall mourn over him. Even so, Amen. I am the Alpha and the Omega, saith **the Lord God**, which is and which was and which is to come, the Almighty. (Revelation 1:7-8 RV) |

But as we see in Revelation 11:17, the reference to the Lord God Almighty includes the descriptor "which art, and wast, and art to come." That is a parallel passage referring back to Jesus Christ in Revelation 1:4 and 1:8. Westcott and Hort knew that is a descriptor of Jehovah. They could not have the revelation that Jesus Christ is Jehovah known. That would mean that Jesus Christ is the eternal Lord God Almighty. Westcott and Hort did not believe Jesus Christ is Jehovah, Lord God Almighty. In Revelation 11:17, Jesus Christ is titled "Lord God Almighty." But the artifice that Westcott and Hort have created excludes Jesus Christ from the title "Lord God Almighty." They needed to include "Lord God" in Revelation 1:8 and say that only refers to God the Father to the exclusion of Jesus Christ. That completes their theological scheme of stripping Jesus Christ of his deity in the Godhead.

> Saying, We give thee thanks, O **Lord God Almighty**, which art, and wast, and art to come; because thou hast taken to thee thy great power, and hast reigned. (Revelation 11:17 AV)

Westcott and Hort had a strange concept of the Godhead. They largely strip Jesus Christ of his place in the Godhead, which explains their removal of 1 John 5:7 in the RV. That is a practice followed by most of the modern Bible versions. Westcott diminishes the divinity of Jesus Christ by claiming that Jesus only had the "substance" of God but was not actually God in "person." That concept was brought into the Revised Version. Westcott explains:

> The passages which have been just quoted throw light upon the doctrine of the Lord's true Divinity (comp. Heb. i. 3, **the very image of his substance, not person as in Authorised Version**). At the same time His true humanity stands out with fresh distinctness in the Revised Version.[91]

The Revised Version (RV) rendered the change so that Jesus Christ is no longer the image of God's person but is instead the image of some nebulous concept called substance, whatever that means. Westcott wanted to make Jesus's humanity stand out by diminishing his deity. The Revised Version of Hebrews 1:3 does not mean that Jesus is God Almighty, a "person" in the Godhead. Instead, the RV has Jesus with some kind of godly substance. That is not the gospel.

| AV | RV |
|---|---|
| Who being the brightness of his glory, and the express image of his **person**, and upholding all things by the word of his power, when he had by himself purged our sins, sat down on the right hand of the Majesty on high. (Hebrews 1:3 AV) | [W]ho being the effulgence of his glory, and the very image of his **substance**, and upholding all things by the word of his power, when he had made purification of sins, sat down on the right hand of the Majesty on high. (Hebrews 1:3 RV) |

# 8 Hebrew Roots Movement Blasphemes Jesus Christ

The Sacred Name movement (a.k.a. Hebrew Roots movement) is founded on the mystical philosophy of the Jewish Kabbalah.[92] Practitioners of the Kabbalah use the names of God as magical incantations to cast "spells" and invoke the power of devils to serve them.[93]

Michael Hoffman explains that "[l]ike the Talmud, the Kabbalah supersedes, nullifies and ultimately replaces the Bible."[94] Lawrence Fine, Professor of Jewish Studies and prominent scholar of medieval Judaism and Jewish mysticism, reveals that the Kabbalah contains the "true" meaning of the Old Testament. The "simple" meaning of the biblical language recedes into the background as the symbolic meaning contained in the Kabbalah supersedes the Bible and takes control. There is a code to the true meaning in the bible that can only be unlocked through the Kabbalah.

> [T]he reader must become accustomed to regarding biblical language in a kabbalistically symbolic way. The Kabbalists taught that the Torah is not only the speech or word of God, but is also the many names of God or expression of God's being.

It is a vast body of symbols, which refers to the various aspects of divine life, the sefirot, and their complex interaction. **The simple meaning of biblical language recedes into the background as symbolic discourse assumes control**. The true meaning of Scripture becomes manifest only when it is read with the proper (sefirotic) code. **Thus the Torah must not be read on the simple or obvious level of meaning; it must be read with the knowledge of a kabbalist who possesses the hermeneutical keys with which to unlock its *inner* truths.**[95]

The Kabbalah at Zohar III, 152a states: "Thus the tales related to the Torah are simply her outer garments, and woe to the person who regards that outer garb as the Torah itself! For such a person will be deprived of a portion in the world to come."[96] That passage in the Kabbalah puts a curse on anyone who tries to read the bible for what it actually says, instead of with the mystical gloss put on it by the Kabbalah.

The Kabbalah is Judaic mystical practices that were adopted by the Jews from Babylon. Mystic and founder of the pantheistic Theosophical Society, H.P. Blavatsky, described the Kabbalah as: "The hidden wisdom of the Hebrew Rabbis of the middle ages derived from the older secret doctrines concerning divine things and cosmogony, which were combined into a theology after the time of the captivity of the Jews in Babylon. All the works that fall under the esoteric category are termed Kabalistic."[97]

The Jewish Encyclopedia acknowledges the Babylonian (a/k/a Chaldean) origins of the Kabbalah (a/k/a Cabala). In addition, the Jewish Encyclopedia explains that Gnosticism flowed from the Jews to the ersatz "Christians." That is yet more authority that Gnosticism flowed from Babylon via the Jewish Gnostics to lay the foundation for the Roman Catholic theology. The esoteric Gnosticism imbued in the Catholic theology was based upon the Jewish Kabbalah.

> The Pythagorean idea of the creative powers of numbers and letters, upon which the "Sefer Yez.irah" is founded, and which was known in tannaitic times . . . is here proved to be an old cabalistic conception. In fact, the belief in the magic power of the letters of the Tetragrammaton and other names of the Deity . . . seems to have originated in Chaldea . . . Whatever, then, the theurgic Cabala was, which, under the name of "Sefer (or "Hilkot" Yez.irah,") induced Babylonian rabbis of the fourth century to "create a calf by magic."

> \* \* \*

> But especially does Gnosticism testify to the antiquity of the Cabala. Of Chaldean origin, as suggested by Kessler . . . and definitively shown by Anz . . . Gnosticism was Jewish in character long before it became Christian.[98]

Magic and occult mysticism runs throughout the Kabbalah. Judith Weill, a professor of Jewish mysticism stated that magic is deeply rooted in Jewish tradition, but the Jews are reticent to acknowledge it and don't even refer to it as magic.[99] Gershom Scholem (1897-1982), Professor of Kabbalah at Hebrew University in Jerusalem, admitted that the Kabbalah contains a great deal of black magic and sorcery, which he explained involves invoking the powers of devils to disrupt the natural order of things.[100] Professor Scholem also stated that there are devils who are in submission to the Talmud; in the Kabbalah these devils are called *shedim Yehuda'im*.[101]

The *Jewish Chronicle* revealed that occult practices such as making amulets, charms, and talismans are taught in Jerusalem at the rabbinic seminary Yeshivat Hamekubalim.[102] That is why Jesus said to the Jews: **"Ye are of your father the devil, and the lusts of your father ye will do."** John 8:44. The bible states clearly that the magic arts are an abomination to the Lord.

> There shall not be found among you any one that maketh his son or his daughter to pass through the fire, or that useth divination, or an observer of times, or an enchanter, or a witch, Or a charmer, or a consulter with familiar spirits, or a wizard, or a necromancer. For all that do these things are an abomination unto the LORD: and because of these abominations the LORD thy God doth drive them out from before thee. (Deuteronomy 18:10-12)

The Kabbalah, like the Talmud, graphically blasphemes Jesus. For example, in Zohar III, 282a, the Kabbalah refers to Jesus as a dog who resides among filth and vermin.[103]

The Hebrew Roots movement has a particular animus toward Jesus. Many in the Hebrew Roots movement (a.k.a., Sacred Name movement) claim that Roman Church officials changed Christ's name from YAHSHUA to JESUS. Dr. James A. Robinson of End Times Issue Ministries is one of many persons, who claims that Jesus' name is a "demonic name" that means "hail Zeus." The "hail Zeus" theory for the name Jesus is endemic in the Sacred Name movement.[104] Robinson claims that Christ's name should be "Yahoosha."[105] It is kind of a free-for-all regarding what Christ's true name should be, whether Yahshua or Yahoosha or any number of similar variants. But one thing they agree on is that "Jesus" is some kind of hybrid Greek/Latin that some of them allege means "Hail Zeus." They claim "this change was made to make [the Roman Catholic] religion more acceptable to the pagan culture. Zeus was chief of the Greco-Roman pantheon of gods, so, according to this theory, the supposed new demigod was easily accepted and Christianity was melded with paganism."[106]

One sect in the Sacred Name free-for-all is the Assembly of the Kingdom of Heaven (AKH). AKH has a variant Hebrew construction for Christ, YaHVaHShooa Ha MASHIACH. AKH explains:

> YaHVaHShooa Ha MASHIACH was born a Jew of the tribe of Yudah. He said, "Salvation is of the Jew." He should therefore have the Jewish name. Jesus on the other hand is a combination of Medo-Grecian name; a combination of IEU and Zeus; a marriage between paganism and christianity--Jesus did not exist till the 1700 AD. YaHVaHShooa is the Truth, the true name of the Son of YaHVaH, ELOHIM. Jesus, on the other hand, is a fake, false and strange name popularised and propagated by religion, a counterfeit--a combination of IEU+ZEUS=IESUS, in AD1700 became Jesus.[107]

Please understand that YaHVaHShooa is not a renaming of Jesus; it is a replacement of Jesus. AKH states that "YaHVaHShua and Jesus are not one, nor the same. ... YaHVaHShooa is the Truth, Jesus is the counterfeit, the false or a lie sown by Satan. ... JESUS CHRIST IS AN OUTRIGHT LIE."[108] (uncials in original)

The House of Yahweh® (HOY) is another Sacred Name organization that denies that Jesus is the Christ.[109] Neither HOY nor any Sacred Name sect is a Christian organization because "[w]hosoever denieth the Son, the same hath not the Father: but he that acknowledgeth the Son hath the Father also." 1 John 2:23.

HOY claims that Christ is Yahshua. HOY claims that Jesus

Christ is an amalgam of the Greek god Zeus and the Hindu god Krishna. HOY claims that those two gods were joined into one deity, Jesus Christ, by a political decree of the Emporer Constantine.

According to HOY, **"Zeus+Krishna=Jesus Christ."**[110] Thus, HOY claims that Jesus Christ is a heathen composite god who must be rejected. Indeed, HOY calls Jesus a "detestable pagan God."[111] Below is a graphic posted on HOY's website depicting HOY's claimed composition of Jesus Christ.

The chosen Christ of the House of Yahweh (HOY) is "Yahshua." Yahshua is not a another name for Jesus, he is a replacement. HOY has stripped Yahshua of his eternal godhood. HOY states that "Yahshua died; Yahshua suffered death, proving by His dying that He was not an immortal, pre-existent Being."[112] HOY's god Yahshua is clearly a different Jesus Christ from the Jesus Christ of the Bible. Jesus is the eternal God Almighty, creator of heaven and earth. "All things were made by him; and without him was not any thing made that was made." John 1:3. "For by him were all things created, that are in heaven, and that are in earth, visible and invisible,." Colossians 1:16. "Behold, a virgin shall be with child, and shall bring forth a son, and they shall call his name Emmanuel, which being interpreted is, **God with us.**" (Matthew 1:23 AV) "I and my Father are one." John 10:30.

> For unto us a child is born, unto us a son is given: and the government shall be upon his shoulder: and his name shall be called Wonderful, Counsellor, The **mighty God, The everlasting Father**, The Prince of Peace. Isaiah 9:6.

We read in Revelation 1:12-13 that Pergamos is the location of "Satan's seat." And what was found in Pergamos? There was a massive temple built to none other than Zeus.[113] So we have it on the authority of God Almighty that Zeus is Satan.

> And to the angel of the church in **Pergamos** write; These things saith he which hath the sharp sword with two edges; I know thy works, and where thou dwellest, even where **Satan's seat** is: and thou holdest fast my name, and hast not denied my faith, even in those days wherein Antipas was my faithful martyr, who was slain among you, where **Satan dwelleth**. (Revelation 2:12-13)

The Hebrew Roots movement is not another kind of Christianity. It is anti-Christian. Those who hold to the mythology that Jesus is Zeus or any other heathen god have committed the unpardonable sin of ascribing to God the characteristics of the devil. Matthew 12:24-32. They are calling Jesus Satan. Their claim that Jesus Christ instead should be replaced with Yahshua is a rejection of Jesus Christ.

Dr. Michael Brown, who has a Ph.D. in Semitic Languages, states that one could argue for the Hebrew Yeshua for Jesus, but there is no authority for "Yahshua." It is a made-up name not supported by any Biblical authority.

81

Why then do some people refer to Jesus as Yahshua? There is absolutely no support for this pronunciation—none at all—and I say this as someone holding a Ph.D. in Semitic languages.[114]

Dr. Brown is mystified by those who would substitute "Yahshua" for Jesus. He addresses the weird and blasphemous claim by some in the Hebrew roots movement that Jesus is a hidden reference to the heathen god Zeus.

What about the alleged connection between the name Jesus (Greek I--esous) and Zeus?

This is one of the most ridiculous claims that has ever been made, but it has received more circulation in recent years (the Internet is an amazing tool of misinformation), and there are some believers who feel that it is not only preferable to use the original Hebrew/Aramaic name, Yeshua, but that it is wrong to use the name Jesus. Because of this, we will briefly examine this claim and expose the fallacies that underlie it.

According to the late A. B. Traina in his Holy Name Bible, "The name of the Son, Yahshua, has been substituted by Jesus, Iesus, and Ea-Zeus (Healing Zeus)."

In this one short sentence, two complete myths are stated as fact: First, there is no such name as Yahshua (as we have just explained), and second, there is no connection of any kind between the Greek name I--esous (or the English name Jesus) and the name Zeus. Absolutely none! You might as well argue that Tiger Woods is the name of a tiger-infested jungle in India as try to connect the name Jesus to the pagan god Zeus. It is that absurd, and it is based on serious linguistic ignorance.[115]

***

Although it is claimed that the Encyclopedia Britannica says that "the name Ieusus (Jesus) is a combination of 2 mythical deities, IEU and SUS (ZEUS, a Greek god)" it actually says no such thing. This is a complete fabrication, intentional or not.

In short, as one Jewish believer once stated, "Jesus is as much related to Zeus as Moses is to mice."

Unfortunately, some popular teachers continue to espouse the Jesus-Zeus connection, and many believers follow the pseudo-scholarship in these fringe, "new revelation" teachings. Not only are these teachings and practices filled with error, but they do not profit in the least.

So, to every English-speaking believer I say: Do not be ashamed to use the name JESUS! That is the proper way to say his name in English—just as Michael is the correct English way to say the Hebrew name mi-kha-el and Moses is the correct English way to say the Hebrew name mo-sheh.[116]

There is no good reason for an English speaker to adopt a different language when preaching the gospel to other English speakers. Such conduct only serves to confuse. And "God is not the author of confusion." 1 Corinthians 14:33. The contrivance of English speakers calling Jesus by a purported Hebrew name is a satanic stratagem to beguile the unlearned and unwary to turn away from the true gospel and true Jesus and follow a different gospel and a different Jesus. See 2 Corinthians 11:4.

Calling our Lord "Jesus" in English is important in light of the passage in the inspired English Holy Bible (KJV) that states emphatically that there is no other name under heaven whereby we must be saved.

> Be it known unto you all, and to all the people of Israel, that **by the name of Jesus Christ of Nazareth**, whom ye crucified, whom God raised from the dead, even by him doth this man stand here before you whole. This is the stone which was set at nought of you builders, which is become the head of the corner. **Neither is there salvation in any other: for there is none other name under heaven given among men, whereby we must be saved.** Acts 410-12.

Yahshua is a different Jesus based on a different gospel warned about in the Bible.

> For if he that cometh preacheth **another Jesus**, whom we have not preached, or if ye receive another spirit, which ye have not received, or **another gospel**, which ye have not accepted, ye might well bear with him. 2 Corinthians 11:4.

God makes it clear that Jesus Christ is Lord. And God has given Jesus a name that is above all names. In the name of Jesus, every knee shall bow, and every tongue will confess that Jesus Christ is Lord.

> Wherefore God also hath highly exalted him, and given him a **name** which is above every name: **That at the name of Jesus every knee should bow**, of things in heaven, and things in earth, and

things under the earth; And that **every tongue should confess that Jesus Christ is Lord**, to the glory of God the Father. Philippians 2:9-11.

A little known fact is that one of the names used for Jesus by the Hebrew roots movement, Yeshu, is used by Jews as a curse against Jesus.[117] Tuvia Pollack, writing for *Kehila Times*, reveals that "the name Yeshu can be seen as an abbreviation of '*Yimach Shmo Uzichro*,' may his name and memory be blotted out."[118] Jesus is regularly cursed in the Jewish Talmud by the name of Yeshu.[119] Indeed, there is an ancient Jewish text that is called the *Sefer Toledot Yeshu,* which presents a blasphemous attack on Jesus by rabbinical Jewish authorities.[120] The *Sefer Toledot Yeshu* alleges that Jesus was an illegitimate child, whose miracles were by means of sorcery, who taught a heretical form of Judaism, seduced women, and died a shameful death.[121]

The Talmud, which calls Jesus Yeshu, as an epithet, is the authoritative religious book in Judaism. The Talmud memorializes the traditions of the Jews. Jesus upbraided the Jews for replacing his laws with their man-made traditions.

> And he said unto them, Full well ye reject the commandment of God, that ye may keep your own tradition. ... Making the word of God of none effect through your tradition, which ye have delivered: and many such like things do ye. (Mark 7:9, 13)

To what traditions was Jesus referring when he upbraided the Pharisees for using them to transgress and replace the laws of God? Can we find out about those traditions today? Yes; the Talmud is a codification of the traditions of the scribes and Pharisees to which Jesus spoke. Michael Rodkinson (M. Levi Frumkin), who wrote the first English translation of the Babylonian Talmud, states the following in his book *The History of the Talmud*:

> Is the literature that Jesus was familiar with in his early years yet in existence in the world? Is it possible for us to get at it? To such inquiries the learned class of Jewish rabbis answer by holding up the Talmud. **The Talmud then, is the written form of that which, in the time of Jesus, was called the Traditions of the Elders**, and to which he makes frequent allusions.[122] (emphasis added)

So we see that the traditions of the Jews are memorialized in the Talmud. During the time of Christ, the Talmud existed only in oral form, which Jesus referred to as the traditions of the scribes and Pharisees. This early oral tradition is called the Mishnah. It was only after Christ's crucifixion that the Mishnah was reduced to writing. The rabbis later added rabbinical commentaries to the Mishnah, which are called the Gemara.[123] Together these comprise the Talmud, which is now a collection of books.

There are today two basic Talmudic texts, the Babylonian Talmud and the Jerusalem Talmud. The Babylonian Talmud is regarded as the authoritative version and takes precedence over the Jerusalem Talmud.[124] The Babylonian Talmud is based on the mystical religious practices of the Babylonians, which the Jewish Rabbis assimilated during their Babylonian captivity around 600 B.C. The Rabbis then used these occult traditions in place of the word of God. In rabbinic Judaism, the Talmud has primacy and authority over God's word in the Old Testament.[125]

According to the Babylonian Talmud, Tractate 'Abodah Zarah, Folio 17a, Christians are allied with hell. Tractate Sanhedrin, Folio 106a curses Jesus. In Tractate Gittin, Folio 57a, Jesus is described as being tormented in boiling hot semen. In Tractate Gittin, Folio 57b, Jesus has been sent to hell, where he is being punished by boiling excrement for mocking the Rabbis. In

Tractate Sanhedrin, Folios 90a and 100b, it states that those who read the gospels are doomed to hell. In Tractate Shabbath, Folio 116a, it states that the New Testament is blank paper and is to be burned. The hatred by Jews against Christ, Christians, and the gospel is so intense that Jews are taught to utter a curse when passing a Christian Church, calling on their heathen god (Hashem) to "destroy this house of the proud."[126]

Rabbi ben Yohai, who believed he was beyond the jurisdiction of God, did not think gentiles were even worthy to live. His views regarding gentiles were that "even the best of gentiles should all be killed."[127] Rabbi ben Yohai is not a rabbi on the fringes of Judaism; he is in fact one of the most revered of rabbis in Judaism; his grave is a shrine in Israel. He authored the Zohar, which is the principle work of the Kabbalah.

The Jews recite *Amidah*, which is a set of eighteen (by some accounts nineteen) weekly Jewish prayers. The twelfth prayer is called *Birkat ha-minim*. The *Birkat ha-minim* is actually a hateful curse against heretics and enemies of the Jews, particularly Christians. The curse was first introduced in the *Amidah* in the first century at Jabneh by Samuel ha Katan, at the request of Rabban Gamaliel II in order to drive followers of Jesus Christ from the synagogues.

The common Jews are as much victims of the Jewish hierarchy as are the Gentiles and Christians. The common Jews are being spiritually brainwashed to the bidding of their rabbis. Jesus explained the process: "Woe unto you, scribes and Pharisees, hypocrites! for ye compass sea and land to make one proselyte, and when he is made, ye make him twofold more the child of hell than yourselves." (Matthew 23:15)

Jews view "Christian" Zionists in the Hebrew Roots movement as "useful idiots," which is a pejorative phrase used by communists to describe Gentile communist propagandists who do not understand the Jewish goals behind communism. Jews have a secret that they keep from the "Christian" Zionists. According to the previously mentioned tractate in the Talmud (*Sanhedrin Folio 90a*), Christians, who are described as those who read the New Testament ("uncanonical books"), have no portion in the world to come.[128] In fact, Jews have a particular hatred for Christians. The hatred by Jews against Christians is so intense that Jews are taught to utter a curse when passing a Christian Church, calling on their heathen god (Hashem) to "destroy this house of the proud."[129] For more information about "Christian" Zionists, read this author's book, *Bloody Zion*.

God warned about just such Jewish machinations, giving rise to Jewish fables and commandments of men that have taken hold in the Hebrew Roots movement.

> For there are many unruly and vain talkers and deceivers, **specially they of the circumcision**: Whose mouths must be stopped, who subvert whole houses, teaching things which they ought not, for filthy lucre's sake. One of themselves, even a prophet of their own, said, The Cretians are alway liars, evil beasts, slow bellies. This witness is true. Wherefore rebuke them sharply, that they may be sound in the faith; **Not giving heed to Jewish fables, and commandments of men, that turn from the truth."** (Titus 1:10-14)

Paul speaks to the Galatians about the very Titus, whom he warned in Titus 1:10-14 about not following Jewish fables. Paul reveals in Galatians 2:2-4 that as a Gentile Christian, Titus was not required to be circumcised according to the custom under the Jewish law. Jesus Christ, as the fulfillment of the promise sealed by circumcision, has freed all who believe in him from the circumcision commandment given to Abraham in Genesis 17:11-12. *See* Romans 4:10-14, Galatians 5:2-11. "Behold, I Paul say

88

unto you, that if ye be circumcised, Christ shall profit you nothing." Galatians 5:12. The false brethren, that is, false Christians, were trying to bring Christians into bondage under the Jewish customs. That is what the Hebrew Roots movement today seeks to do.

> And I went up by revelation, and communicated unto them that gospel which I preach among the Gentiles, but privately to them which were of reputation, lest by any means I should run, or had run, in vain. But **neither Titus, who was with me**, being a Greek, was compelled to be circumcised: **And that because of false brethren unawares brought in, who came in privily to spy out our liberty which we have in Christ Jesus, that they might bring us into bondage:** (Galatians 2:2-4)

Paul upbraided Peter for doing some of the same things the Hebrew Roots movement promote. Jesus fulfilled the law. We are saved by God's Grace through faith in Jesus Christ, not by obedience to the ceremonial laws of the Old Testament.

> But when Peter was come to Antioch, I withstood him to the face, because he was to be blamed. For before that certain came from James, he did eat with the Gentiles: but when they were come, he withdrew and separated himself, **fearing them which were of the circumcision**. And the other **Jews dissembled likewise with him**; insomuch that **Barnabas also was carried away with their dissimulation**. But when I saw that **they walked not uprightly according to the truth of the gospel**, I said unto Peter before them all, If thou, being a Jew, livest after the manner of Gentiles, and not as do the Jews, **why compellest thou the Gentiles to live as do the Jews?** We who are Jews

by nature, and not sinners of the Gentiles, Knowing that **a man is not justified by the works of the law, but by the faith of Jesus Christ**, even we have believed in Jesus Christ, that we might be justified by the faith of Christ, and not by the works of the law: for **by the works of the law shall no flesh be justified.** (Galatians 2:11-16)

Paul made it clear in Galatians 5:2-4 that we are to stand in the liberty God has given us. Once one is born again, there is no need for circumcision. Paul states, by the inspiration of God, that if one gets circumcised, that is evidence that they are seeking to be justified by the law. That person has "fallen from grace."

Stand fast therefore in the liberty wherewith Christ hath made us free, and be not entangled again with the yoke of bondage. **Behold, I Paul say unto you, that if ye be circumcised, Christ shall profit you nothing.** For I testify again to every man that is circumcised, that he is a debtor to do the whole law. **Christ is become of no effect unto you,** whosoever of you are justified by the law; ye are fallen from grace. (Galatians 5:1-4)

Lo and behold, what does the Hebrew Roots movement advocate? Circumcision! Tim Kelley, writing for *Al Yisrael*, which is "a Hebrew Roots Fellowship," argues that for Christians, "physical circumcision is still a very important part of God's law."[130] *119 Ministries* is yet another Hebrew Roots organization. It states: "We believe that we are to teach all nations to obey the Torah (Law of God)."[131] *119 Ministries* argues that while circumcision is not required for salvation, Christians should be circumcised in obedience to the law.[132]

This movement calling for circumcision is not new. The Book of Acts reveals:

Forasmuch as we have heard, that certain which went out from us have troubled you with words, subverting your souls, saying, Ye must be circumcised, and keep the law: to whom we gave no such commandment: (Acts 15:24)

Why are Christians allowed not to get circumcised? The answer is that once one believes in Jesus Christ, he is circumcised inwardly. There is no need for an outward circumcision.

For he is not a Jew, which is one outwardly; neither is that circumcision, which is outward in the flesh: But he is a Jew, which is one inwardly; and circumcision is that of the heart, in the spirit, and not in the letter; whose praise is not of men, but of God. Romans 2:28-29.

The purpose of the law was to bring us to Christ. Once Christ redeems us by his grace through faith in Jesus Christ, we are no longer under the law. The law is then written in our inward parts. We obey because Christ works through us.

But before faith came, we were kept under the law, shut up unto the faith which should afterwards be revealed. Wherefore the law was our schoolmaster to bring us unto Christ, that we might be justified by faith. But after that faith is come, we are no longer under a schoolmaster. For ye are all the children of God by faith in Christ Jesus. (Galatians 3:23-26 AV)

Another name variant for Jesus' name used by many Hebrew Roots movement adherents is Yeshua. They have been taught that, as a Jew, Jesus' actual name in Hebrew should be Yeshua. Jews indeed render Jesus' name in Hebrew as Yeshua.

The Tree of Life Version (TLV) of the Bible is marketed as "a translation created to highlight the Jewish roots of the Christian faith."[133] It replaces Jesus with *Yeshua*. Where in English it states that at the name of Jesus every knee shall bow, the TLV changes it to say that in the name of *Yeshua* every knee shall bow. The average English speaker hearing the name of *Yeshua* would not know who *Yeshua* is. And that is the idea behind the TLV and the Hebrew Roots movement.

| KJV | TLV |
|---|---|
| Wherefore God also hath highly exalted him, and given him a name which is above every name: That at the name of **Jesus** every knee should bow, of things in heaven, and things in earth, and things under the earth; And that every tongue should confess that **Jesus Christ is Lord**, to the glory of God the Father. (Philippians 2:9-11 KJV) | For this reason God highly exalted Him and gave Him the name that is above every name, that at the name of *Yeshua* every knee should bow, in heaven and on the earth and under the earth, and every tongue profess that *Yeshua* **the Messiah is Lord**—to the glory of God the Father. (Philippians 2:9-11 TLV) (italics in original) |

Notice that the KJV passage says that **"every tongue should confess that Jesus Christ is Lord."** Tongue, in that context, is a word pregnant with meaning. Tongue not only means "[s]peech; words or declarations,"[134] it also means "[a] language; the whole sum of words used by a particular nation. The English tongue...."[135] The Bible distinguishes people by their different tongues (i.e., languages). "I will gather all nations and tongues." Isaiah 66:18.

The TLV has an agenda. It selectively chose to only change the English name for **Jesus** to the Hebrew *Yeshua*. Notably, when it comes to other Jewish names, the TLV sticks with the English rendering and does not change them to the Hebrew tongue. For example, the TLV of Acts 7:14 states: "So **Joseph** sent and called for **Jacob** and all his relatives—seventy-five persons. (Acts 7:14 TLV) The Hebrew name for Joseph is *Yosef,*[136] and the Hebrew name for Jacob is *Yaakov.*[137] However, the TLV does not render their names in Acts 7:14 in Hebrew; instead, it renders them as the English names Joseph and Jacob. But the TLV uses a different rule when it comes to Jesus. The TLV, which purports to be an English translation of the Bible, changed the Lord's name in English (Jesus) to the Hebrew *Yeshua.*

Philippians 2:9-11 informs us that every person will confess that Jesus Christ is Lord in his native tongue. The TLV of Philippians of 2:11 is a strange amalgam of Hebrew (*Yeshua*), Anglicized Hebrew (the Messiah), and English (Lord). Neither a Hebrew speaker nor an English speaker would say *"Yeshua the Messiah is Lord"* as rendered in the TLV of Philippians 2:11. A Hebrew speaker would confess that *Yeshua HaMashiach hoveh Adonai*, and an English speaker would confess that Jesus Christ is Lord.

An English speaker will not confess in the foreign language of Hebrew *Yeshua HaMashiach hoveh Adonai*. But the TLV suggests that an English speaker will confess partly in Hebrew by calling Jesus *Yeshua*. Indeed, the TLV of Philippians 2:11 uses the English Lord instead of the Hebrew Adonai, thus revealing that it is arbitrary and capricious in its use of Hebrew names and titles for God. An English speaker's tongue is English, not Hebrew. It is a contrived affectation for an English speaker to adopt a Hebrew name (*Yeshua*) for Jesus. Hebrew is a foreign tongue not understood by an English speaker. The King James Bible passage in Philippians 2:9-11 impeaches the Hebrew Roots movement's adoption of the Hebrew *Yeshua* in place of the English Jesus. English speakers adopting a Hebrew title for Jesus is part of a nefarious plan to Judaize the gospel.

The TLV is an English Bible, yet it tells English speakers to speak Hebrew when confessing that Jesus Christ is Lord in Philippians 1:9-11. The TLV instructs English speakers that they must confess not that Jesus Christ is Lord but that "*Yeshua* the Messiah is Lord." In Philippians 1:9-11 the TLV uses the anglicized Hebrew "the Messiah" instead of the English "Christ." But in Acts 4:10-12, the TLV uses the Hebrew *ha-Mashiach* instead of the anglicized Hebrew "the Messiah" or English "Christ." According to the TLV, English speakers must understand that there is no other name under heaven by which we must be saved but *Yeshua ha-Mashiach ha-Natzrati*. The problem is that most English speakers do not know what that means. That English Bible passage in the TLV is not English but Hebrew. It is a foreign language to an English speaker. It is not understandable; it is confusing. "God is not the author of confusion." 1 Corinthians 14:33. Indeed, The TLV tries to reverse what God did at Pentecost, where God ensured that "every man heard them speak in his own language." *See* Acts 2:1-5. God intends for people to get his inspired gospel in their language. A person must receive the gospel in his tongue for him to understand the gospel. The gospel presented in a foreign tongue leaves the recipient without understanding, i.e., without inspiration.

| KJV | TLV |
|---|---|
| Be it known unto you all, and to all the people of Israel, that **by the name of Jesus Christ of Nazareth**, whom ye crucified, whom God raised from the dead, even by him doth this man stand here before you whole. This is the stone which was set at nought of you builders, which is become the head of the corner. **Neither is there salvation in any other: for there is none other name under heaven given among men, whereby we must be saved.** (Acts 410-12 KJV) | [L]et it be known to all of you and to all the people of Israel, that by the name of *Yeshua  ha-Mashiach  ha-Natzrati*—whom you had crucified, whom God raised from the dead—this one stands before you whole. This *Yeshua* is 'the stone—rejected by you, the builders—that has become the chief cornerstone.' **There is salvation in no one else, for there is no other name under heaven given to mankind by which we must be saved!** (Acts 4:10-12 TLV) (italics in original) |

As previously explained, Jews often drop the "a" and call him Yeshu, which is an epithet against him. The practice of English speakers to call Jesus Yeshua is part of a sinister scheme. It is a devilish stratagem by Judaizers to corrupt the gospel of grace.

The religion of the Jews is a mixture that, on the surface, appears godly but is, in fact, a wholly leavened loaf of heathenism. "Then Jesus said unto them, Take heed and beware of the leaven of the Pharisees and of the Sadducees. . . . Then understood they how that he bade them not beware of the leaven of bread, but of the doctrine of the Pharisees and of the Sadducees." (Matthew 16:6, 12)  Paul also warned about the Judaizers who were trying to inject their Judaic doctrine into the church. He warned: "A little leaven leaveneth the whole lump." (Galatians 5:9)

Changing Jesus' name to Yeshua is a subtle way to change the doctrines of the gospel. Rabbi Mordecai Griffin founded Lapid Judaism, which is part of the Hebrew Roots movement. Rabbi Griffin reveals that changing the English Jesus into the Hebrew Yeshua is to change who the Messiah is. Changing Christ's name in English from the English Jesus to the Hebrew Yeshua is a trick by the subtle serpent (see Genesis 3:1) to substitute a false Jesus (called Yeshua) for the true Jesus of the gospel, just as Paul warned would happen in 2 Corinthians 11:4. Rabbi Griffin let the cat out of the bag and disclosed that Yeshua of the Hebrew Roots movement is NOT Jesus. He states that Jesus means nothing.

> When we say that we beleive in Yeshua as the Messiah is THAT the same thing as saying that we believe in "Jesus"?? Yeshua means "salvation". Yehoshua (the longer form of the Messiah's Name) means "HaShem Saves." The name Jesus literally means nothing. It has no meaning what-so-ever.[138]

Rabbi Griffin reveals that calling the Messiah (Christ) Yeshua is for the purpose of bringing Christians back under the yoke of the Jewish law. Rabbi Griffin states:

> Lapid Judaism exists to restore the original faith of Yeshua, the Messiah of Israel. Our mission and vision is to restore Yeshua-centered Judaism to the world. To accomplish this mission, we intend to bring complete and lasting transformation by making true disciples, strengthen families, building communities and proclaiming Yeshua as Messiah expressed in an authentically Jewish Torah observant lifestyle.[139]

When Rabbi Griffin uses the word Torah he is including also the traditions of the Jews memorialized in the Talmud.

Lapid Judaism is referred to as an "Orthodox" Jewish movement because it adheres to Jewish practice and observance within the guidelines of Talmudic law and its codifiers.[140]

Lapid Judaism is a way to corrupt the gospel of grace and change it into subjugation under Orthodox Hassidic (a.k.a., Chassidic) Judaism.

Lapid Judaism, as a movement, is defined as Yeshua-Centered Judaism. It is a return, restoration and revival of the original faith of Moshiach and His Talmidim (disciples). Lapid is a tradition with its roots in the Orthodox tradition and its soul linked to the Chassidic movement.[141]

Hassidic Judaism is Phariseeism. Indeed, Rabbi Griffin reveals that the Yeshua of Lapid Judaism is a Pharisee.

Jesus the Pharisee? Was Jesus (actually It's Yeshua) from the Pharisees? Yeshua the Messiah was a Pharisee. He taught as a Pharisee, lived as a Pharisee, affirmed the religious practice of the Pharisees, and supported both the Written and Oral Torah as a Pharisee.[142]

What more proof does one need to understand that Yeshua of the Hebrew Roots movement is NOT the Jesus of the Bible? Changing Jesus' name to Yeshua is a change in who Jesus is. Yeshua of the Hebrew Roots movement is a devilish Pharisee. Jesus Christ of the gospel states his unequivocal opinion about the Pharisees that they are vipers and children of hell.

But woe unto you, scribes and Pharisees, hypocrites! for ye shut up the kingdom of heaven against men: for ye neither go in yourselves, neither suffer ye them that are entering to go in. Woe unto you, scribes and Pharisees, hypocrites! for ye devour widows' houses, and for a pretence make long prayer: therefore ye shall receive the greater damnation. Woe unto you, scribes and Pharisees, hypocrites! for ye compass sea and land to make one proselyte, and when he is made, ye make him twofold more the child of hell than yourselves. Woe unto you, ye blind guides, ... Ye fools and blind: ... Ye fools and blind: ... Woe unto you, scribes and Pharisees, hypocrites! ... Woe unto you, scribes and Pharisees, hypocrites! ... Thou blind Pharisee, ... Woe unto you, scribes and Pharisees, hypocrites! for ye are like unto whited sepulchres, which indeed appear beautiful outward, but are within full of dead men's bones, and of all uncleanness. Even so ye also outwardly appear righteous unto men, but within ye are full of hypocrisy and iniquity. Woe unto you, scribes and Pharisees, hypocrites!... Ye serpents, ye generation of vipers, how can ye escape the damnation of hell? (Matthew 23:13-33)

The Hebrew Roots movement is a satanic attack on Jesus Christ. This author was sharing Christian tracts that I had prepared with someone who had contacted me. He was passing out the tracts. But in an email, he suddenly asked for the tracts to be in an editable format so that he could change Jesus to "Yahusha."

I responded, in pertinent part:

Absolutely NOT! You want to replace Jesus with Yahusha because you reject Jesus. [... You] stated, "Jesus has no meaning in Hebrew nor in English." Thus, Yahusha is not a different name for Jesus Christ; Yahusha is a replacement for Jesus Christ.

That means that Yahusha is NOT Jesus Christ.
You have rejected Jesus Christ. ... You are a
devotee of the Hebrew Roots Movement, which is
Jewish heathenism. Changing Jesus' name to
Yahusha or Yeshua is a subtle way to change the
doctrines of the gospel.[143]

That person responded by sending me an email with the
following message: "jesus is satan 666 gee zi sigma."[144] That
statement reveals the underlying theology of the Hebrew Roots
movement. I responded to that email by explaining to him:

Did you just say "Jesus is Satan"? That is the
unforgivable sin! Jesus explains in Matthew
12:24-32 that to attribute to God the characteristics
of the devil is the unpardonable sin of blaspheming
the Holy Spirit.[145]

He replied with an email containing a series of graphics
prepared by one of the many Hebrew Roots movement websites
that distinguished Jesus Christ from "Yahusha Messiah."[146] One
of the graphics stated: "Yahusha Messiah came from heaven,
became flesh was born of a virgin and came from the tribe of
Judah and spoke Hebrew." The tract also stated: "Jesus Christ did
not come from heaven, was not the Son of Yahuwah and did not
die for our sins on a tree." Thus, according to the Hebrew Roots
movement "Yahusha Messiah" is not another name for Jesus
Christ; "Yahusha Messiah" is another god. It gets worse; the
graphics equated Jesus Christ with Baphomet.

The statements by the email writer reveal that Yahusha and
the other variants of Jesus in the Hebrew Roots movement are not
different Hebrew renderings of Jesus. Those words are
replacements of Jesus. They blaspheme Jesus. The Hebrew Roots
movement preaches the different Jesus about whom the Apostle
Paul warned in 2 Corinthians 114. Calling Jesus Satan is the

unforgivable sin. Jesus explains in Matthew 12:24-32 that to attribute to God the characteristics of the devil is the unpardonable sin of blaspheming the Holy Spirit. Those who remain in the Hebrew Roots movement are accursed, just as Paul warned in Galatians 1:8: "But though we, or an angel from heaven, preach any other gospel unto you than that which we have preached unto you, let him be accursed." The logical conclusion of the graphics cited by the email correspondent is that the Hebrew Roots movement considers Jesus Christ to be Baphomet (i.e., Satan). Indeed, that is the conclusion to which the email correspondent came.

The Hebrew Roots movement is based on the principles in the blasphemous Jewish Kabbalah, which is the foundation of Phariseeism. The Pharisees were principally behind the crucifixion of Jesus Christ. Recall, in Matthew 12:24 it was the Pharisees who claimed that Jesus Christ was using the power of Beelzebub to cast out devils.

> But when the Pharisees heard it, they said, This fellow doth not cast out devils, but by Beelzebub the prince of the devils. ... Wherefore I say unto you, All manner of sin and blasphemy shall be forgiven unto men: but the **blasphemy against the Holy Ghost shall not be forgiven unto men.** And whosoever speaketh a word against the Son of man, it shall be forgiven him: but **whosoever speaketh against the Holy Ghost, it shall not be forgiven him, neither in this world, neither in the world to come.** Matthew 12:24, 31-32.

The Pharisees were the first to be recorded in the Scriptures as committing the unforgivable sin. The Pharisees have not changed; they continue to blaspheme the Holy Spirit through the Kabbalistic Hebrew Roots movement.

Please understand that not all those in the Hebrew Roots movement have committed the unforgivable sin. It is only those who have sunk to such a degree of spiritual depravity to attribute to Jesus Christ the characteristics of the devil who have committed the unforgivable sin. English speakers hoodwinked into calling Jesus Christ Yahoosha, Yahusha, Yahshua, YaHVaHShooa, Yeshua, or Yeshu have not committed an unpardonable sin. But to call Jesus Christ Satan is an unforgivable sin. Why would anyone take part in a movement that portrays itself as "Christian" yet whose leadership rejects and blasphemes Jesus Christ and even calls him Satan?

# 9 The Israel of God

The Hebrew Roots movement views physical Israel as the ultimate object of God's plan. But they do not understand the gospel. Jesus Christ is Israel. We find in Matthew 2:13-15 that when Jesus was brought out of Egypt after fleeing from Herod, it fulfilled the prophecy in Hosea 11:1, wherein God prophesied that he would call his son out of Egypt. In Hosea, we learn that the son God called out of Egypt was Israel. Hence, Jesus Christ is Israel.

> And when they were departed, behold, the angel of the Lord appeareth to Joseph in a dream, saying, Arise, and take the young child and his mother, and flee into Egypt, and be thou there until I bring thee word: for Herod will seek the young child to destroy him. When he arose, he took the young child and his mother by night, and departed into Egypt: **And was there until the death of Herod: that it might be fulfilled which was spoken of the Lord by the prophet, saying, Out of Egypt have I called my son.** (Matthew 2:13-15)

When we read the prophecy in Hosea 11:1, we find that Jesus fulfilled the prophecy of Israel being called out of Egypt.

God states in Hosea 11:1 that he loved Israel and called Israel, his son, out of Egypt. "When Israel was a child, then I loved him, and called my son out of Egypt." Hosea 11:1. Jesus fulfilled that prophecy. Jesus Christ is Israel.

We know, according to the gospel, that Jesus is God's "firstborn" Son.

> For by him were all things created, that are in heaven, and that are in earth, visible and invisible, whether they be thrones, or dominions, or principalities, or powers: all things were created by him, and for him: And he is before all things, and by him all things consist. **And he is the head of the body, the church: who is the beginning, the firstborn from the dead; that in all things he might have the preeminence.** (Colossians 1:16-18)

And who does God also identify as his firstborn? The answer is Israel. "And thou shalt say unto Pharaoh, Thus saith the LORD, Israel is my son, even my firstborn:" (Exodus 4:22) There can only be one firstborn. Thus, Jesus Christ is Israel.

Hebrews 8:1-10:39 makes explicitly clear that Christ fulfilled the requirements of the law by sacrificing himself once for sins for all time. If the blood of animals were sufficient to satisfy God there would be no need for him to come to the earth and sacrifice himself. "But now hath he obtained a more excellent ministry, by how much also he is the mediator of a better covenant, which was established upon better promises. For if that first covenant had been faultless, then should no place have been sought for the second." (Hebrews 8:6-7)

> So Christ was **once offered** to bear the sins of many; and unto them that look for him shall he

appear the second time without sin unto salvation. (Hebrews 9:28)

> By the which will we are sanctified through the offering of the body of Jesus Christ **once for all**. And every priest standeth daily ministering and offering oftentimes the same sacrifices, which can never take away sins: But this man, after he had **offered one sacrifice for sins for ever**, sat down on the right hand of God; From henceforth expecting till his enemies be made his footstool. For **by one offering he hath perfected for ever them that are sanctified**. (Hebrews 10:10-14)

God would not have us return to the weak and beggarly elements of the Old Testament law. *See* Galatians 4:9-11. To teach such a thing is to blasphemously state that Christ's sacrifice was imperfect and insufficient, and that therefore there is a need to reinstate the animal sacrifices. The Old Testament law was to act as a schoolmaster until the promise of Christ. God would have no reason to reinstate something that was intended to be in place only until he came to offer his own body as a perfect sacrifice. In Christ there is neither Jew nor Gentile, we are all one by faith in Christ. He is not going to divide us once again into Jew and Gentile. His church is his body which cannot be divided. 1 Corinthians 1:13. A kingdom divided against itself cannot stand. Mark 3:24.

God has not cast away Israel. His Israel is made up of those whom he foreknew before the foundation of the world who would believe in Jesus unto salvation. Therefore, all Israel shall be saved.

> God hath not cast away his people which he foreknew. (Romans 11:2) And so **all Israel shall be saved**. (Romans 11:26)

104

It is important for God's heirs to know who they are. His heirs are those who have the faith of Abraham, not those that have the flesh of Abraham.

> Even as Abraham believed God, and it was accounted to him for righteousness. Know ye therefore that they which are of faith, the same are the children of Abraham. And the scripture, foreseeing that God would justify the heathen through faith, preached before the gospel unto Abraham, saying, In thee shall all nations be blessed. **So then they which be of faith are blessed with faithful Abraham.** (Galatians 3:6-9)

Fleshly Israel is nor to inherit the promises of God; it is those who are chosen and justified by his sovereign grace who are his heirs and not those who are born of the flesh of Abraham. **"That being justified by his grace, we should be made heirs according to the hope of eternal life."** (Titus 3:7) It is not fleshly Israel, who are the children of the flesh, who are the chosen of God; it is the children who have faith in Jesus Christ who are the children of the promise, the true Israel of God, that are the seed of Abraham.

In Christ there is neither Jew nor Gentile, we are all one by faith in Christ. He is not going to divide us once again into Jew and Gentile. His church is his body which cannot be divided. 1 Corinthians 1:13. For a kingdom divided against itself cannot stand. Mark 3:24. The seed of the promises to Abraham is Christ and those who have the faith of Christ, his church, not fleshly Israel.

> But before faith came, we were kept under the law, shut up unto the faith which should afterwards be revealed. Wherefore the law was our schoolmaster to bring us unto Christ, that we might be justified

by faith. **But after that faith is come, we are no longer under a schoolmaster**. For ye are all the children of God by faith in Christ Jesus. For as many of you as have been baptized into Christ have put on Christ. **There is neither Jew nor Greek, there is neither bond nor free, there is neither male nor female: for ye are all one in Christ Jesus. And if ye be Christ's, then are ye Abraham's seed, and heirs according to the promise.** Galatians 3:23-29.

A Jew who believes in Jesus as Christ becomes a new creation. He is no longer a fleshly Jew. He becomes a spiritual Jew, a Christian. "For in Christ Jesus neither circumcision availeth any thing, nor uncircumcision, but a new creature." Galatians 6:15.

The Bible makes clear that the old covenant made to fleshly Israel has vanished away, being replaced by the new covenant of faith in Jesus Christ. "In that he saith, A new covenant, he hath made the first old. Now that which decayeth and waxeth old is ready to vanish away." (Hebrews 8:13) Why would God reinstate something in which he has said would vanish away and in which he has had no pleasure? "In burnt offerings and sacrifices for sin thou hast had no pleasure." Hebrews 10:6.

Fleshly Israel is symbolized by the fig tree. That fig tree will never again bear fruit.

And seeing a fig tree afar off having leaves, he came, if haply he might find any thing thereon: and when he came to it, he found nothing but leaves; for the time of figs was not yet. And Jesus answered and said unto it, **No man eat fruit of thee hereafter for ever.** And his disciples heard it. . . . And in the morning, as they passed by, they saw the fig tree dried up from the roots. And Peter calling to remembrance saith unto him, Master, behold, the fig tree which thou cursedst is withered away. Mark 11:13-14, 20-21.

Spiritual Israel is symbolized by the olive tree. "Can the fig tree, my brethren, bear olive berries? either a vine, figs? so can no fountain both yield salt water and fresh." James 3:12. The answer is no! Fleshly Israel will never ever bear spiritual fruit for God. The spiritual fruit only comes from the spiritual olive plant, the church.

As we have already seen, the blessings of God do not flow to the physical seed of Abraham but rather to his spiritual seed. We know that Jesus is the seed of Abraham. Galatians 3:16. All who believe in Jesus are heirs of the promise given to Abraham. Galatians 3:23-29. Obedience to God is the result of salvation, not the cause of it. Ephesians 2:8-10. Just as with Abraham, who believed God and it was accounted to him as righteousness, so too for all others who believe God it is also accounted unto them as righteousness. Galatians 3:6-9.

A true Jew is the spiritual seed of Abraham, not the physical seed. "For he is not a Jew, which is one outwardly; neither is that circumcision, which is outward in the flesh: But he is a Jew, which is one inwardly; and circumcision is that of the heart, in the spirit, and not in the letter; whose praise is not of men, but of God." Romans 2:28-29. "Not as though the word of God hath taken none effect. For they are not all Israel, which are of Israel: Neither, because they are the seed of Abraham, are they all children: but, In Isaac shall thy seed be called. That is, They which are the children of the flesh, these are not the children of God: but the children of the promise are counted for the seed." Romans 9:6-8.

The eternal blessings of Abraham flow to all who believe in Jesus Christ. God's kingdom is a spiritual kingdom, not an earthly kingdom. His children are spiritual children, not earthly children. In God's kingdom there are no distinctions between Jew or Gentile. "There is neither Jew nor Greek, there is neither bond nor free, there is neither male nor female: for ye are all one in Christ Jesus. And if ye be Christ's, then are ye Abraham's seed, and heirs according to the promise." Galatians 3:28-29.

Fleshly Israel of the Old Testament is a temporal type of the spiritual Israel of the New Testament, which is the church.

But with many of them God was not well pleased: for they were overthrown in the wilderness. **Now these things were our examples, to the intent we should not lust after evil things, as they also lusted.** 1 Corinthians 10:5-6.

**Now all these things happened unto them for ensamples: and they are written for our admonition, upon whom the ends of the world are come.** 1 Corinthians 10:11.

Thus, the prophecies regarding Israel had both temporal and spiritual fulfillments. The distinction between the temporal Israel and the eternal Israel is explained clearly in R. B. Yerby's book *The Once and Future Israel*. First there is the temporal earthly fulfillment and then there is the spiritual fulfillment. 1 Corinthians 15:46.

The scriptures teach us that in all of God's dealings with mankind, from the time of Adam, we may discern the same divine principle at work, namely, "first the natural, then the spiritual." (1 Cor 15:45-46) God has progressively revealed his purpose through, first, his dealings with the natural Israel and, second and finally, his dealings with spiritual Israel. (There is no scriptural basis for the

108

regressive idea that God's dealings will again be centered exclusively on natural Israel at some future date.)

Because God's dealings follow the sequence of first the natural, then the spiritual, it is easy to see and understand that the same progression applied to his people and his promises. The natural people of Old Testament Israel enjoyed the natural fulfillment of the promises made to them, and saw the promises invalidated through sin and unbelief. Likewise, the spiritual people of New Testament Israel, the followers of Jesus Christ, have received, are receiving and will receive all spiritual fulfillments of the promises.

* * *

[In Galatians 4:21-31] as in many other New Testament passages, Paul skillfully defeated his adversaries with their own ammunition. He took the "foolish Galatians" who desired to be under the law (Gal 4:21) right into the thick of Old Testament Law, into Genesis, the first book of Moses, to prove a spiritual truth with natural types. The early church recognized the need for spiritual authority to support their doctrines (for them, of course, the scriptures were the writings we today call the Old Testament) and therefore, under the inspiration of the Holy Spirit, they quoted freely from the Old Testament.

In the fourth chapter of Galatians, as elsewhere, Paul proved his point through the superior understanding God gave him of the true meaning of the Old Testament scriptures. He said that the story of the two sons of Abraham was more than just a prominent part of the history of the Jewish people. It was, he said, an allegory (Gal. 4:24), that is, a story in which the people and events were symbols or types standing for some greater truth (Gal. 4:24).

The allegory speaks of two women and their two sons who were fathered by Abraham. Hagar, the bondwoman and the mother of Ishmael who was "born after the flesh" (Gal 4:23), typifies natural Jerusalem. Sarah, the freewoman and the mother of Isaac, the child of promise (Gal 4:23, 28), typifies the church which is spiritual Jerusalem. The children of natural Jerusalem are in bondage (Gal. 4:25), as are all who are unsaved, but the children of the church, the heavenly Jerusalem, are free (Gal. 4:26). Those who are in bondage, who are not born again are only "born after the flesh" (Gal. 4:29) cannot possibly be God's people. Therefore, the scriptures "cast out"(Gal 4:30) the natural Jerusalem and her children after the flesh, and identify the heirs as the believers in Christ who are the children of promise (Gal 4:30).

* * *

Paul was constantly in trouble with the Jews because his spiritual interpretations of the Old Testament scriptures warred with their natural interpretation. Our onetime Pharisee had come to see clearly that "the things that are seen are temporal, but the things which are not seen are eternal" (2 Cor 4:18) but his former colleagues could not believe that their highly vaunted institutions were ready to "vanish away" (Heb

8:13).

* * *

Because the Lord Jesus "endured the cross, despising the shame" (Heb 12:2) spiritual Israel hears a better voice than the voices heard by natural Israel (Heb. 1:1, 2), and we have, among other things, a better Priest (Heb. 4:15), a better priesthood (Heb. 5:6), a better hope (Heb. 7:19), a better covenant (Heb. 8:10), a better Tabernacle (Heb. 9:11), a better altar (Heb. 13:10), a better sacrifice (Heb. 9:14), a better country (Heb. 11:16), and a better city (Heb. 12:22).[147]

Many believe that some of the prophecies in the Old Testament regarding natural Israel have not been fulfilled and therefore there must be a post-Christian period during which they will be fulfilled. Let us examine these Old Testament prophecies. In Genesis 12:2 God told Abraham: "And I will make of thee a great nation, and I will bless thee, and make thy name great; and thou shalt be a blessing." Abraham did not see the fulfillment of that prophecy. That promise was fulfilled in part by fleshly Israel. "And God spake unto Israel in the visions of the night, and said, Jacob, Jacob. And he said, Here am I. And he said, I am God, the God of thy father: fear not to go down into Egypt; for **I will there make of thee a great nation**" Genesis 46:2-3. After 400 years of captivity, God raised up Moses who brought Israel out of Egyptian bondage and it became a great nation, just as promised by God. See Joshua 8-12; 1 Chronicles 17:21.

Keep therefore and do them; for this is your wisdom and your understanding in the sight of the nations, which shall hear all these statutes, and say, **Surely this great nation is a wise and understanding people. For what nation is there**

111

**so great, who hath God so nigh unto them, as the LORD our God is in all things that we call upon him for? And what nation is there so great, that hath statutes and judgments so righteous as all this law, which I set before you this day?** (Deuteronomy 4:6-8)

There was yet to be a spiritual fulfillment of the promise that from Abraham would spring a great nation. The church was the spiritual fulfillment of the promise given to Abraham.

> **But ye are a chosen generation, a royal priesthood, an holy nation, a peculiar people**; that ye should shew forth the praises of him who hath called you out of darkness into his marvellous light: Which in time past were not a people, but are now the people of God: which had not obtained mercy, but now have obtained mercy. 1 Peter 2:9-10.

On three different occasions God promised that Abraham's descendants would be too numerous to count.

> And I will make thy seed as the dust of the earth: so that if a man can number the dust of the earth, then shall thy seed also be numbered. Genesis 13:16.

> And he brought him forth abroad, and said, Look now toward heaven, and tell the stars, if thou be able to number them: and he said unto him, So shall thy seed be. Genesis 15:5.

> That in blessing I will bless thee, and in multiplying I will multiply thy seed as the stars of the heaven, and as the sand which is upon the sea

shore; and thy seed shall possess the gate of his enemies; Genesis 22:17.

Was that promise fulfilled in part by temporal Israel? Yes! We have the proof of the God inspired testimony of Moses, Solomon, and the author of Hebrews.

Now, O LORD God, let thy promise unto David my father be established: for **thou hast made me king over a people like the dust of the earth in multitude.** 2 Chronicles 1:9.

**The LORD your God hath multiplied you, and, behold, ye are this day as the stars of heaven for multitude.** Deuteronomy 1:10.

**Therefore sprang there even of one, and him as good as dead, so many as the stars of the sky in multitude, and as the sand which is by the sea shore innumerable.** Hebrews 11:12.

**Judah and Israel were many, as the sand which is by the sea in multitude**, eating and drinking, and making merry. 1 Kings 4:20.

There was to be a future spiritual fulfillment of that promise through the church. The seed of Abraham is a spiritual seed. The nation that would spring from him would be a nation built not on fleshly Israel only. There would be a better fulfillment of the promise through faith.

Therefore it is of faith, that it might be by grace; to the end the promise might be sure to all the seed; not to that only which is of the law, but to that also which is of **the faith of Abraham; who is the father of us all**. Romans 4:16.

In Genesis 17:5, God told Abraham he would be a father of many nations.

> (As it is written, **I have made thee a father of many nations**,) before him whom he believed, even God, who quickeneth the dead, and calleth those things which be not as though they were. Romans 4:17.

As Abraham believed the promises of God and God counted it as righteousness, so too is it with those who have the faith of Abraham; they are the spiritual seed of Abraham. The church of God is the promised spiritual great nation.

> Who against hope believed in hope, that he might become the father of many nations, according to that which was spoken, **So shall thy seed be.** Romans 4:18.

Those that believe in Christ are Abraham's seed and the innumerable children that God promised Abraham. Galatians 3:29. First came the temporal earthly fulfillment of the promise through natural Israel, then came the spiritual eternal fulfillment through the church of Christ.

On no fewer than four different occasions God promised to Abraham and his descendants the land of Canaan. Genesis 12:7; 13:14-15; 15:7,18; 17:8. Many say that the promise of the land was not fulfilled. That is not true. God has stated clearly that all the land that he promised to fleshly Israel was given to them.

> **And the LORD gave unto Israel all the land which he sware to give unto their fathers; and they possessed it, and dwelt therein.** And the LORD gave them rest round about, according to all that he sware unto their fathers: and there stood not

a man of all their enemies before them; the LORD delivered all their enemies into their hand. **There failed not ought of any good thing which the LORD had spoken unto the house of Israel; all came to pass.** Joshua 21:43-45.

Some claim that the land that Israel occupied did not reach all the way from Egypt to the river Euphrates, as promised by God in Genesis 15:18, and therefore there is to be a future fulfillment of the promise. That claim is simply not true. Solomon, King of Israel, ruled from the river Euphrates to Egypt. "And Solomon reigned over all kingdoms from **the river unto the land of the Philistines, and unto the border of Egypt:** they brought presents, and served Solomon all the days of his life." 1 Kings 4:21. Is the river mentioned in verse 21 the Euphrates? Yes it is! In verse 24 we read that Solomon had dominion over Tipsah. Tipsah was located on the Euphrates in Mesopotamia. "For he had dominion over all the region on this side the river, from Tiphsah even to Azzah, over all the kings on this side the river: and he had peace on all sides round about him." 1 Kings 4:24.

Some have tried to beguile the children of God by stating that because Genesis 17:7-9 states that the land of Canaan was to be an everlasting possession of Israel, it is God's plan that natural Israel regain possession of that land. Let us look at that passage.

> **And I will establish my covenant between me and thee and thy seed after thee in their generations for an everlasting covenant, to be a God unto thee, and to thy seed after thee. And I will give unto thee, and to thy seed after thee, the land wherein thou art a stranger, all the land of Canaan, for an everlasting possession; and I will be their God. And God said unto Abraham, Thou shalt keep my covenant therefore, thou, and thy seed after thee in their**

**generations.** (Genesis 17:7-9)

The key passage is found in Genesis 17:9. It states: "And God said unto Abraham, Thou shalt keep my covenant therefore, thou, and thy seed after thee in their generations." A covenant is a mutual agreement. Each party has promised to do something. What many miss is that God has set forth both his promise and Abraham's promise. In Genesis 17:1 God tells Abraham "walk before me, and be thou perfect." Genesis 17:1. In return God promises to "be a God unto thee, and thy seed after thee." Genesis 17:7. How could Abraham be perfect? God provided a way for Abraham to keep his end of the bargain.

God supplied Abraham with faith. That faith was counted as perfect righteousness for Abraham. "Abraham believed God, and it was counted unto him for righteousness." (Romans 4:3) Abraham did not have the capacity to believe God (Ephesians 2:1), so God supplied the faith. The faith of Abraham was a gift from God. Ephesians 2:8. Jesus is the "author and finisher" of Abraham's faith and indeed the faith of all of the elect of God. Hebrews 2:2.

God fulfilled the requirements of both sides of the covenant he made with Abraham. That is what God meant when he said in Genesis 17:9: "And God said unto Abraham, **Thou shalt keep my covenant** therefore, thou, and thy seed after thee in their generations." God ensured that Abraham would keep his end of the agreement and "be perfect" by supplying Abraham's faith that was accounted unto him for perfect righteousness. God stated that Abraham's seed after him would keep the covenant. God ensures the perfection of his seed by supplying the faith that is accounted unto them for righteousness. John 6:37, 65; 17:2.

Salvation is not based upon anything intrinsically good in Abraham, it is based upon the intrinsic goodness and grace of God. Faith in Jesus Christ is accounted for righteousness. That faith is a gift of God (Romans 4) according to his sovereign will (Ephesians 1-2) without regard to the lineage or merit of his chosen (John 1:12-13).

The passage in Genesis 17:1-9 refers to an everlasting covenant. That everlasting covenant is the New Covenant of Christ, which is fulfilled in Christ. It is a spiritual covenant. The land promised is a heavenly land that will be "everlasting." God himself has revealed that truth to those who have ears to hear and eyes to see.

By faith Abraham, when he was called to go out into a place which he should after receive for an inheritance, obeyed; and he went out, not knowing whither he went. By faith he sojourned in the land of promise, as in a strange country, dwelling in tabernacles with Isaac and Jacob, the heirs with him of the same promise: **For he looked for a city which hath foundations, whose builder and maker is God.** Through faith also Sara herself received strength to conceive seed, and was delivered of a child when she was past age, because she judged him faithful who had promised. Therefore sprang there even of one, and him as good as dead, so many as the stars of the sky in multitude, and as the sand which is by the sea shore innumerable. **These all died in faith, not having received the promises**, but having seen them afar off, and were persuaded of them, and embraced them, and confessed that they were strangers and pilgrims on the earth. For they that say such things declare plainly that they seek a country. And truly, if they had been mindful of that country from whence they came out, they might have had opportunity to have returned. **But now they desire a better country, that is, an**

**heavenly:** wherefore God is not ashamed to be called their God: for he hath prepared for them a city. (Hebrews 11:8-16)

Notice that those pilgrims of God died in faith not having received the promises on earth. The everlasting covenant of God is spiritual, the land is eternal in heaven, not temporal on earth. For the earthly land of Canaan could not possibly be an everlasting possession of fleshly Israel, because the earth will one day be destroyed and replaced by a new heaven and a new earth. "Looking for and hasting unto the coming of the day of God, wherein the heavens being on fire shall be dissolved, and the elements shall melt with fervent heat? Nevertheless we, according to his promise, look for new heavens and a new earth, wherein dwelleth righteousness." (2 Peter 3:12-13) "And I saw a new heaven and a new earth: for the first heaven and the first earth were passed away; and there was no more sea." (Revelation 21:1)

God made a conditional covenant with Israel that is referred to as the Mosaic covenant. The blessings were conditioned on the obedience of Israel. Israel violated that covenant and therefore the blessings did not flow to fleshly Israel.

Now therefore, if ye will obey my voice indeed, and keep my covenant, then ye shall be a peculiar treasure unto me above all people: for all the earth is mine: And ye shall be unto me a kingdom of priests, and an holy nation. These are the words which thou shalt speak unto the children of Israel. And Moses came and called for the elders of the people, and laid before their faces all these words which the LORD commanded him. And all the people answered together, and said, All that the LORD hath spoken we will do. And Moses returned the words of the people unto the LORD. (Exodus 19:5-8)

Notice that "all the people answered together, and said, All that the LORD hath spoken we will do." Exodus 19:8. In this covenant the Jews agreed to fulfill the requirements of the covenant by their own effort. Further, notice that God did not say that they "shalt keep my covenant" as he said to Abraham in Genesis 17:9. God promised that Abraham would keep the covenant. In Exodus 19:8, however, the Jews promised to keep the covenant. God is showing us in these two different covenants, the difference between the futility of attempted salvation by the works of man and the solidity of salvation by the grace of God. No sooner did the Jews agree to obey God in Exodus 19:8 than they immediately fell into idolatry.

> Saying unto Aaron, Make us gods to go before us: for as for this Moses, which brought us out of the land of Egypt, we wot not what is become of him. And they made a calf in those days, and offered sacrifice unto the idol, and rejoiced in the works of their own hands. Then God turned, and gave them up to worship the host of heaven; as it is written in the book of the prophets, O ye house of Israel, have ye offered to me slain beasts and sacrifices by the space of forty years in the wilderness? Yea, ye took up the tabernacle of Moloch, and the star of your god Remphan, figures which ye made to worship them: and I will carry you away beyond Babylon. (Acts 7:40-43)

The history of natural Israel is one of continual sin intermixed with periods of repentance, until God finally finished with them according to his foreordained plan. There is a spiritual Israel, the church, to whom the blessings flow. God's true Israel is and always was the church. The church contains the children of the promise. "Now we, brethren, as Isaac was, are the children of promise." (Galatians 4:28) The church is the Israel of God. "For in Christ Jesus neither circumcision availeth any thing, nor uncircumcision, but a new creature. And as many as walk according to this rule, peace be on them, and mercy, and upon the **Israel of God.**" (Galatians 6:15-16) The church is the temple of God. "Know ye not that ye are **the temple of God**, and that the Spirit of God dwelleth in you?" (1 Corinthians 3:16) The church is God's holy nation inheriting the promises made by God in Exodus 19:5-8. **"But ye are a chosen generation, a royal priesthood, an holy nation, a peculiar people**; that ye should shew forth the praises of him who hath called you out of darkness into his marvellous light." (1 Peter 2:9)

God does not have a plan of salvation for fleshly Israel that is any different from the plan of salvation he has for Gentiles. Salvation is by grace through faith in Jesus Christ for all. There is one body of Christ, his spiritual Israel, made up of Gentiles and the remnant of fleshly Israel.

> Even when we were dead in sins, hath quickened us together with Christ, (by grace ye are saved;) And hath raised us up together, and made us sit together in heavenly places in Christ Jesus: That in the ages to come he might shew the exceeding riches of his grace in his kindness toward us through Christ Jesus. For by grace are ye saved through faith; and that not of yourselves: it is the gift of God: Not of works, lest any man should boast. For we are his workmanship, created in Christ Jesus unto good works, which God hath before ordained that we should walk in them. Wherefore remember, that ye being in time past Gentiles in the flesh, who are called Uncircumcision by that which called the Circumcision in the flesh made by hands; That at that time ye were without Christ, being aliens from the commonwealth of Israel, and strangers from the covenants of promise, having no hope, and

without God in the world: But now in Christ Jesus ye who sometimes were far off are made nigh by the blood of Christ. **For he is our peace, who hath made both one, and hath broken down the middle wall of partition between us; Having abolished in his flesh the enmity, even the law of commandments contained in ordinances; for to make in himself of twain one new man, so making peace; And that he might reconcile both unto God in one body by the cross, having slain the enmity thereby: And came and preached peace to you which were afar off, and to them that were nigh.** For through him we both have access by one Spirit unto the Father. Now therefore ye are no more strangers and foreigners, but fellowcitizens with the saints, and of the household of God; And are built upon the foundation of the apostles and prophets, Jesus Christ himself being the chief corner stone; In whom all the building fitly framed together groweth unto an holy temple in the Lord: In whom ye also are builded together for an habitation of God through the Spirit. (Ephesians 2:5-22)

Christ did not in any way provide some exclusive plan for the Jews. He stated that the gospel was to be preached to "all nations." Luke 24:47. The only difference for the Jews was that the preaching of the gospel should start at Jerusalem. Romans 1:16; Acts 18:5-6. It was to start with the Jews, but that does not mean it is to end with the Jews in some post-Christian era. The Old Testament has prophecies of the church of God consisting of both believing Jews and Gentiles. Amos 9:11-12; Hosea 1:10; 2:23. The Old Testament prophecies regarding salvation to both the Jews and Gentiles together are explained in Acts 15:13-17; 26:22-23; Romans 9:23-26; and 1 Peter 2:10.

Jesus is Israel (Matthew 2:13-15, Hosea 11:1, Colossians 1:16-18, Exodus 4:22), and all believers are in Jesus and Jesus is in us (John 17:21-23). Thus, all believers make up spiritual Israel, the Israel of God, the church.

> **That they all may be one; as thou, Father, art in me, and I in thee, that they also may be one in us**: that the world may believe that thou hast sent me. And the glory which thou gavest me I have given them; **that they may be one, even as we are one: I in them, and thou in me, that they may be made perfect in one;** and that the world may know that thou hast sent me, and hast loved them, as thou hast loved me. (John 17:21-23 AV)

> **Believest thou not that I am in the Father, and the Father in me?** the words that I speak unto you I speak not of myself: but the Father that dwelleth in me, he doeth the works. Believe me that **I am in the Father, and the Father in me**: or else believe me for the very works' sake. ...At that day ye shall know that **I am in my Father, and ye in me, and I in you.**" (John 14:10-11, 20)

Jesus is the head of the church, which is the body of Christ. Colossians 1:18, I Corinthians 12:27. The New Testament writers, being inspired by God, clearly understood that the church is the Israel of God and is the object of the promises made to Israel by God in the Old Testament.[148]

> **Paul said that believers are:**

"The children of God" (Romans 8:16).
"The Household of God" (Ephesians 2:19).
"The children of Abraham" (Colossians 3:7).
"Abraham's seed" (Galatians 3:29).

."The Children of promise" (Rom. 9:8, Galatians 4:28).
"A peculiar people" (Titus 2:14).
"The elect of God" (Colossians 3:12).
"Heirs of God"(Rom. 8:17).
"Heirs according to the promise" (Galatians 3:29).
"The temple of God" (1 Cor 3:16).
"The circumcision" (Philippians 3:3).
"The Israel of God" (Galatians 6:16).

**Peter said that believers are:**

"A chosen generation" (1 Peter 2:9).
"A royal priesthood" (1 Peter 2:9).
"A holy nation" (1 Peter 2:9).
"A peculiar people" (1 Peter 2:9).

**James said that believers are:**

"Heirs of the kingdom" (James 2:5).

**John said that believers are:**

"The sons of God" (John 1:12).
"Kings and priests unto God" (Revelation 1:6).
"The new Jerusalem" (Revelation 3:12).
"The Holy city (Revelation 21:2).

**The letter to the Hebrews said that believers are:**

"The people of God" (Hebrews 4:9).
"Mount Sion" (Hebrews 12:22).
"The city of the living God" (Hebrews 12:22).
"The heavenly Jerusalem" (Hebrews 12:22).

The Jews are our enemies, because they are antichrist. Romans 11:28. Jews hate Christ and Christians. Those that are born after the flesh will always persecute those born after the spirit. Galatians 4:29. The spiritual children of God, however, are to love them and pray for them. "But I say unto you which hear, Love your enemies, do good to them which hate you, Bless them that curse you, and pray for them which despitefully use you." (Luke 6:27-28) God has chosen a remnant of Jews for salvation. We should preach the gospel to the lost world, including the Jews. We, however, should not think that a Jew is any different in God's plan than a Catholic, a Muslim, a Hindu, a Buddhist, a Satanist or any other follower of one of Satan's heathen religions.

Salvation for all, is by the grace of God through faith in Jesus Christ. If a Jew repents of his antichrist religion and believes in Jesus, then he is saved. Once saved, a Jew will not continue in his Talmudic practices any more than a Catholic will continue his Catholic practices or a Satanist will continue his satanic practices once they are saved. All believers in Christ become spiritual Jews, which are Christians. Romans 2:28-29.

Loving our enemies does not mean that we should condone the pagan practices of the Jews, Catholics, Muslims, or other heathens. Rather, we are called by God to reprove them. "And have no fellowship with the unfruitful works of darkness, but rather reprove them." (Ephesians 5:11)

# Endnotes

1.Nick Sayers, Revelation 16:5 and the Triadic Declaration, A defense of the reading of "shalt be" in the Authorized Version, at 12, October 2016. See also Should יהוה be Translated as Yahweh or LORD? - Psalm 110:1 | Dr. James White, Ocotber 5, 2020, https://www.youtube.com/watch?v=fDgogzOrxis.

2.KJV Debate: James White & Thomas Ross: King James Bible Only & Textus Receptus Modern Versions & LSB, KJB1611, March 10, 2023, https://www.youtube.com/watch?v=9RgZ-mUh3LM.

3.KJV Debate: James White & Thomas Ross: King James Bible Only & Textus Receptus Modern Versions & LSB, KJB1611, March 10, 2023, https://www.youtube.com/watch?v=9RgZ-mUh3LM.

4.Legacy Standard Bible Exposed (Full Video), January 27, 2022, https://www.youtube.com/watch?v=X-V9zuHqRyA.

5.Legacy Standard Bible Exposed (Full Video), January 27, 2022, https://www.youtube.com/watch?v=X-V9zuHqRyA.

6.Gail Riplinger, In Awe of Thy Word, at 806 (2003).

7.Chris R. Armstrong, Master of language: Lancelot Andrewes, https://christianhistoryinstitute.org/magazine/article/master-of-language-lancelot-andrewes (last visited on December 28, 2023).

8.The King James Bible Translators, https://thekingsbible.com/Library/KJVTranslators (last visited on December 28, 2023).

9.The King James Translators, https://kingjamesbibletranslators.org/ (last visited on December 28, 2023).

10.John Hinton, Ridiculous KJV Bible Corrections: Who is Yahweh?, https://av1611.com/kjbp/ridiculous-kjv-bible-corrections/Yahweh-Jehova-YHVH.html (last visited on November 16, 2023).

11.The Divine Names and Titles, Appendix 4 To The Companion Bible, https://www.therain.org/appendixes/app4.html (last visited in November 19, 2023).

12.Nick Sayers, Revelation 16:5 and the Triadic Declaration, A defense of the reading of "shalt be" in the Authorized Version, at 13, October 2016.

13.Schaff-Herzog Enclyclopedia, Yahweh, at 472, https://ccel.org/ccel/schaff/encyc12/encyc12.y.html (last visited on November 14, 2023).

14.Schaff-Herzog Enclyclopedia, Yahweh, at 472, https://ccel.org/ccel/schaff/encyc12/encyc12.y.html (last visited on November 14, 2023).

15.Schaff-Herzog Enclyclopedia, Yahweh, at 470, https://ccel.org/ccel/schaff/encyc12/encyc12.y.html (last visited on November 14, 2023).

16.Schaff-Herzog Enclyclopedia, Yahweh, at 472, https://ccel.org/ccel/schaff/encyc12/encyc12.y.html (last visited on November 14, 2023).

17.Miller, James M.; Hayes, John H. A History of Ancient Israel and Judah. Westminster John Knox Press, at 109-110 (1986). ISBN 978-0-664-21262-9. https://www.google.com/books/edition/A_History_of_Ancient_Israel_and_Judah/uDijjc_D5P0C?hl=en&gbp v=1&pg=PA110&printsec=frontcover.

18.Betz, Arnold Gottfried (2000). "Monotheism". In Freedman, David Noel; Myer, Allen C. (eds.). Eerdmans Dictionary of the Bible. Eerdmans. ISBN 978-90-5356-503-2. https://www.google.com/books/edition/Eerdmans_Dict ionary_of_the_Bible/qRtUqxkB7wkC?hl=en&gbpv=1 &bsq=bible+monotheism+Betz&pg=PA917&printsec =frontcover.

19.Calvin's Commentaries, Vol. 1: Genesis, Part I, tr. by John King, [1847-50], https://sacred-texts.com/chr/calvin/cc01/cc01007.htm# fr_108. (last visited on November 20, 2023).

20.Nehemia Gordon, The Vowels of Yehovah and Yahweh, June 30, 2023, https://www.youtube.com/watch?v=JYBqEjt1iiU.

21.Nehemia Gordon, The Vowels of Yehovah and Yahweh, June 30, 2023, https://www.youtube.com/watch?v=JYBqEjt1iiU.

22.Nehemia Gordon, The Vowels of Yehovah and Yahweh, June 30, 2023, https://www.youtube.com/watch?v=JYBqEjt1iiU.

23.The Historical Origins of Yahweh, Nehemia Gordon Clips, September 15, 2023, https://www.youtube.com/watch?v=gG5jeuPyxBs&t=8 0s.

24. The Historical Origins of Yahweh, Nehemia Gordon Clips, September 15, 2023, https://www.youtube.com/watch?v=gG5jeuPyxBs&t=80s.

25. Gesenius' Hebrew and Chaldee Lexicon of the Old Testament Scriptures, at CCCXX XVII.

26. Gesenius' Hebrew and Chaldee Lexicon of the Old Testament Scriptures, at CCCXX XVII.

27. The Historical Origins of Yahweh, Nehemia Gordon Clips, September 15, 2023, https://www.youtube.com/watch?v=gG5jeuPyxBs&t=80s.

28. Daniel E. Fleming, Yahweh before Israel: Glimpses of History in a Divine Name, Cambridge University Press, at 230, 2020.

29. Israel Knohl, Hovav the Midianite: Why Was the End of the Story Cut?, https://www.thetorah.com/article/hovav-the-midianite-why-was-the-end-of-the-story-cut (last visited on December 2, 2023).

30. Israel Knohl, Hovav the Midianite: Why Was the End of the Story Cut?, https://www.thetorah.com/article/hovav-the-midianite-why-was-the-end-of-the-story-cut (last visited on December 2, 2023), citing Rainer Albertz, A History of Israelite Religion in the Old Testament Period, vol. 1 (trans. J. Bowden; London: OTL, 1994), 49-55. The aversion to the Midianites apparent in some of the biblical traditions stems, it seems, from the tensions between priestly houses; see Frank. M. Cross, From Epic to Canon (Baltimore: Johns Hopkins Press, 1998),

59-63.

31.What is the Meaning of the Divine Name Yahweh?,
New International Version,
https://www.thenivbible.com/blog/what-does-yahweh-
mean-in-the-bible/ (last visited on December 2, 2023).

32.The Meaning of God's Name, Nehemia Gordon
Clips, September 15, 2023,
https://www.youtube.com/watch?v=4vgXMmBst8w&l
ist=WL&index=9.

33.Israel Knohl, YHWH: The Original Arabic Meaning
of the Name,
https://www.thetorah.com/article/yhwh-the-original-ara
bic-meaning-of-the-name (last visited on December 2,
2023)..

34.John Hinton, Ridiculous KJV Bible Corrections:
Who is Yahweh?,
https://av1611.com/kjbp/ridiculous-kjv-bible-correctio
ns/Yahweh-Jehova-YHVH.html (last visited on
November 16, 2023).

35.Gail Riplinger, In Awe of Thy Word, at 421 (2003).

36.Gail Riplinger, In Awe of Thy Word, at 415 (2003).

37.Gail Riplinger, In Awe of Thy Word, at 416 (2003).

38.Gail Riplinger, In Awe of Thy Word, at 417 (2003).

39.John Hinton, Ridiculous KJV Bible Corrections:
Who is Yahweh?,
https://av1611.com/kjbp/ridiculous-kjv-bible-correctio
ns/Yahweh-Jehova-YHVH.html (last visited on
November 16, 2023).

40. About Dr. Nehemia Gordon, PhD, Nehemia's Wall, https://www.nehemiaswall.com/about-nehemia-gordon (last visited on November 18, 2023).

41. Nehemia Gordon, Hebrew Voices #66 – The Historical Pronunciation of Vav, February 28, 2018, https://www.nehemiaswall.com/historical-pronunciation-vav. Also found at: The Pronunciation of the Hebrew Letter Vav (Nehemia Gordon), September 16, 2016, https://www.youtube.com/watch?v=0td4d2UGP0k&t=524s.

42. Is Jeff A. Benner in the "Gunsights" of The LORD ?, November 20, 2022, https://aramaicjudaizers.blogspot.com/2018/07/is-jeff-benner-in-gunsights-of-lord.html.

43. The Way of Yahweh (Part1 of 5), April 28, 2010, https://www.youtube.com/watch?v=rfP6yNbU61A.

44. Nehemia Gordon, Hebrew Voices #66 – The Historical Pronunciation of Vav, February 28, 2018, https://www.nehemiaswall.com/historical-pronunciation-vav. Also found at: The Pronunciation of the Hebrew Letter Vav (Nehemia Gordon), September 16, 2016, https://www.youtube.com/watch?v=0td4d2UGP0k&t=524s.

45. Nehemia Gordon, Hebrew Voices #66 – The Historical Pronunciation of Vav, February 28, 2018, https://www.nehemiaswall.com/historical-pronunciation-vav. Also found at: The Pronunciation of the Hebrew Letter Vav (Nehemia Gordon), September 16, 2016, https://www.youtube.com/watch?v=0td4d2UGP0k&t=524s.

46.See, e.g., Nehemia Gordon on the Pronunciation of the Letter Vav, https://ancient-hebrew.org/ancient-alphabet/vav-discussion.htm (last visited on November 18, 2023).

47.Bible and a Bicycle, Understanding the Hebrew language featuring Jeff Benner, August 15, 2023, https://www.youtube.com/watch?v=XWc6Q5RAeAM. The Way of Yahweh (Part1 of 5), April 28, 2010, https://www.youtube.com/watch?v=rfP6yNbU61A.

48.See Vav, https://ancient-hebrew.org/ancient-alphabet/vav.htm (last visited on November 14, 2023). Jeff A. Benner, Ancient Hebrew Alphabet - Lesson 6 - Vav, April 10, 2013, https://www.youtube.com/watch?v=Ota0EAf2iQM.

49.Thomas Ross, The Battle Over the Inspiration of the Hebrew Vowel Points, Examined Particularly As Waged in England, https://faithsaves.net/history-hebrew-vowel-points/ (last visited on December 26, 2023).

50.God's name is not Yahweh – Proof from Jewish Rabbis, A Rood Awakening, October 31, 2017, https://www.youtube.com/watch?v=yeeA_Abd5Nk.

51.Nehemia Gordon, 1,000 Manuscripts with Yehovah, January 25, 2018, https://www.youtube.com/watch?v=DA3VKpVP17U.

52.John Gill, A Dissertation Concerning the Antiquity of the Hebrew Language, Letters, Vowel Points, and Accents, 1767. https://www.areopage.net/Gill.pdf.

53. Jot, Online Etymology Dictionary, https://www.etymonline.com/search?q=jot (last visited on November 16, 2023).

54. Tittle, Online Etymology Dictionary, https://www.etymonline.com/search?q=tittle (last visited on November 16, 2013).

55. Tittle, YourDictionary, https://www.yourdictionary.com/tittle (last visited on November 16, 2023).

56. Diacritic, Collins English Dictionary, https://www.collinsdictionary.com/dictionary/english/diacritic (last visited on November 16, 2023).

57. John Gill, A Dissertation Concerning the Antiquity of the Hebrew Language, Letters, Vowel Points, and Accents, 1767, at 89. https://www.areopage.net/Gill.pdf.

58. Thomas Ross, The Battle Over the Inspiration of the Hebrew Vowel Points, Examined Particularly As Waged in England, https://faithsaves.net/history-hebrew-vowel-points/ (last visited on December 26, 2023).

59. Thomas Ross, The Battle Over the Inspiration of the Hebrew Vowel Points, Examined Particularly As Waged in England, https://faithsaves.net/history-hebrew-vowel-points/ (last visited on December 26, 2023).

60. Whitfiield, Peter, A Dissertation on the Hebrew Vowel-Points, showing that they are an original and essential part of the Language. Liverpool, 1748, https://kjvgalatians220.files.wordpress.com/2012/03/a-

dissertation-on-the-hebrew-vowel-points-etc.pdf.

61.Dr. Thomas M. Strouse, A Review of and
Observations about Peter Whitfield's "A Dissertation
on the Hebrew Vowel-Points," Emmanuel Baptist
Theological Seminary,
https://studylib.net/doc/7593895/strouse-on-peter-whitf
ield--vowel-points (last visited on December 28, 2023).

62.Dr. Thomas M. Strouse, A Review of and
Observations about Peter Whitfield's "A Dissertation
on the Hebrew Vowel-Points," Emmanuel Baptist
Theological Seminary,
https://studylib.net/doc/7593895/strouse-on-peter-whitf
ield--vowel-points (last visited on December 28, 2023).

63.Dr. Thomas M. Strouse, A Review of and
Observations about Peter Whitfield's "A Dissertation
on the Hebrew Vowel-Points," Emmanuel Baptist
Theological Seminary,
https://studylib.net/doc/7593895/strouse-on-peter-whitf
ield--vowel-points (last visited on December 28, 2023).

64.Paul Henebury, Autographa & Apographa: John
Owen on Inspiration and Preservation, 20 January
2013,
https://drreluctant.wordpress.com/2013/01/20/autograp
ha-apographa-john-owen-on-inspiration-and-preservati
on/.

65.The Works of John Owen, D.D., Volume 1X,
Divine Original of Scripture. The Integrity and Purity
of the Hebrew and Greek Text, Edited by William M.
Goold and Charles W. Quick (1865).

66.The Works of John Owen, D.D., Volume 1X,
Divine Original of Scripture. The Integrity and Purity

of the Hebrew and Greek Text, Edited by William M.
Goold and Charles W. Quick, at 90 (1865).

67. The Works of John Owen, D.D., Volume 1X,
Divine Original of Scripture. The Integrity and Purity
of the Hebrew and Greek Text, Edited by William M.
Goold and Charles W. Quick, at 89 (1865).

68. The Works of John Owen, D.D., Volume 1X,
Divine Original of Scripture. The Integrity and Purity
of the Hebrew and Greek Text, Edited by William M.
Goold and Charles W. Quick, at 89 (1865).

69. Scott Clark, Helvetic Consensus Formula (1675),
Translated by Martin I. Klauber, September 1, 2022,
https://heidelblog.net/2012/09/helvetic-consensus-form
ula-1675/.

70. Legacy Standard Bible Exposed (Full Video),
January 27, 2022,
https://www.youtube.com/watch?v=X-V9zuHqRyA.

71. John Hinton, Ridiculous KJV Bible Corrections:
Who is Yahweh?,
https://av1611.com/kjbp/ridiculous-kjv-bible-correctio
ns/Yahweh-Jehova-YHVH.html (last visited on
November 16, 2023).

72. Nehemia Gordon, Hebrew Voices #66 – The
Historical Pronunciation of Vav, February 28, 2018,
https://www.nehemiaswall.com/historical-pronunciatio
n-vav. Also found at: The Pronunciation of the Hebrew
Letter Vav (Nehemia Gordon), September 16, 2016,
https://www.youtube.com/watch?v=0td4d2UGP0k&t=
524s. Jeff A. Benner knows Dr. Gordon's opinion.
Benner maintains that *vav* originally took on the
"waw" sound. He states that the "v" sound is a modern

Hebrew form. Benner is unwilling to budge on his opinin that vav originally had a "w" sound even when faced with proof that he is wrong. See, e.g., Nehemia Gordon on the Pronunciation of the Letter Vav, https://ancient-hebrew.org/ancient-alphabet/vav-discussion.htm (last visited on November 18, 2023). Benner's opinion is skewed by his belief that God's name is Yahweh. The Way of Yahweh (Part1 of 5), April 28, 2010, https://www.youtube.com/watch?v=rfP6yNbU61A. It seems that Benner has an agenda to maintain the myth that the original pronunciation for *vav* is "w." See Vav, https://ancient-hebrew.org/ancient-alphabet/vav.htm (last visited on November 14, 2023). Jeff A. Benner, Ancient Hebrew Alphabet - Lesson 6 - Vav, April 10, 2013, https://www.youtube.com/watch?v=Ota0EAf2iQM.

73. John Hinton, Ridiculous KJV Bible Corrections: Who is Yahweh?, https://av1611.com/kjbp/ridiculous-kjv-bible-corrections/Yahweh-Jehova-YHVH.html (last visited on November 16, 2023).

74. Theophoric Names, https://www.putoffthyshoes.com/seminary (last visited on December 27, 2023).

75. Theophoric Names, https://www.putoffthyshoes.com/seminary (last visited on December 27, 2023).

76. The Meaning of God's Name, Nehemia Gordon Clips, September 15, 2023, https://www.youtube.com/watch?v=4vgXMmBst8w&list=WL&index=9.

77.Nick Sayers, Revelation 16:5 and the Triadic Declaration, A defense of the reading of "shalt be" in the Authorized Version, at 12, October 2016.

78.Brooke Foss Westcott, Some Lessons of the Revised Version of the New Testament, at 204-05 (1897).

79.Brooke Foss Westcott, Some Lessons of the Revised Version of the New Testament, at 184-85 (1897).

80.Arthur Fenton Hort, Life and Letters of Fenton John Anthony Hort, Vol. II, at 138-39 (1896).

81.Arthur Fenton Hort, Life and Letters of Fenton John Anthony Hort, Vol. I, at. 250 (1896).

82.Mike Leake, On Those Missing Verses In Your ESV and NIV Bible, July 14, 2015, https://www.mikeleake.net/2015/07/on-those-missing-verses-in-your-esv-and-niv-bible.html.

83.The New Athenians.

84.F. J. A. Hort, The Apocalypse of St. John 1-3, with Introduction, Commentary, and Additional Notes, http://www.westcotthort.com/bookshelf.html (last visited on December 12, 2023).

85.You Call *This* a Heresy? The Views of Arius, In His Own Words, The Bart Ehrman Blog, April 25, 2021, https://ehrmanblog.org/the-actual-heretical-views-of-arius-in-his-own-words/.

86.You Call *This* a Heresy? The Views of Arius, In His Own Words, The Bart Ehrman Blog, April 25,

2021,
https://ehrmanblog.org/the-actual-heretical-views-of-ar
ius-in-his-own-words/.

87.White, James R. The King James Only
Controversy: Can You Trust the Modern Translations?
(1995), quoted in pertinent part by Peter S. Ruckman,
The Scholarship Only Controversy, at 111 (1996).

88.Everlasing, American Dictionary of the English
Language,
https://webstersdictionary1828.com/Dictionary/everlast
ing (last visited on December 12, 2023).

89.D. A. Waite, The Theological Heresies of Westcott
and Hort, As Seen in Their Own Writings, The Bible
for Today, 1979,
https://faithsaves.net/heresies-westcott-hort/.

90.F. J. A. Hort, The Apocalypse of St. John 1-3, with
Introduction, Commentary, and Additional Notes,
http://www.westcotthort.com/bookshelf.html (last
visited on December 12, 2023).

91.Brooke Foss Westcott, Some Lessons of the
Revised Version of the New Testament, at 201 (1897).

92.Doublemindedness in the Hebrew Roots Movement
– The Use of Kabbalah and Gematria, October 24,
2008,
https://joyfullygrowingingrace.wordpress.com/2008/10
/24/doublemindedness-in-the-hebrew-roots-movement-
the-use-of-kabbalah-and-gematria/. Esoteric Hebrew
Names of God,
https://www.hebrew4christians.com/Names_of_G-d/Es
oteric/esoteric.html (last visited on November 16,
2023).

93.Esoteric Hebrew Names of God, https://www.hebrew4christians.com/Names_of_G-d/Es oteric/esoteric.html (last visited on November 16, 2023).

94.Michael Hoffman, *Judaism Discovered*, at 785 (2008).

95.Lawrence Fine, Chapter on Kabbalistic Texts, From: *Back to the Sources: Reading the Classic Jewish Texts* ("The First Complete Modern Guide to the Great Books of the Jewish Tradition: What They Are and How to Read Them"), at p. 337 (2006) (bold emphasis added, italics in original).

96.Lawrence Fine, Chapter on Kabbalistic Texts, From: *Back to the Sources: Reading the Classic Jewish Texts* ("The First Complete Modern Guide to the Great Books of the Jewish Tradition: What They Are and How to Read Them"), at p. 337 (2006) (quoting Zohar III, 152a).

97.Blavatsky, Theosophical Glossary, p. 168 (quoted by Barbara Aho, Mystery, Babylon the Great Catholic or Jewish?, at http://watch.pair.com/mystery-babylon.html#cabala (last visited on April 17, 2010)).

98.Jewish Encyclopedia, Cabala, at http://www.jewishencyclopedia.com/view.jsp?artid=1 &letter=C#4 (last visited on April 18, 2010).

99.MICHAEL A. HOFFMAN, JUDAISM'S STRANGE GODS, at p. 88, (2000).

100.MICHAEL A. HOFFMAN, JUDAISM'S STRANGE GODS, at p. 88, (2000). See also Michael

Hoffman, *Judaism Discovered*, at 779 (2008) (quoting Gershom Scholem, *Kabbalah* pp.183-84).

101.MICHAEL A. HOFFMAN, JUDAISM'S STRANGE GODS, at p. 91, (2000).

102.Michael Hoffman, *Judaism Discovered*, at 780 (2008) (quoting Helen Jacaobus, *Eye Jinx*, Jewish Chronicle, May 7, 1999).

103.MICHAEL A. HOFFMAN, JUDAISM'S STRANGE GODS, at p. 92, (2000).

104.What is the real name of the Messiah, http://hiddenbible.com/jesuszeus/jesuszeus.html (last visited on November 17, 2023).

105.James A. Robinson, Jesus means "Hail Zeus" and is a pagan, that is, Demonic name -- his name is Yahooshua, December 3, 2022, https://www.eti-ministries.org/jesus-means-hail-zeus-and-is-a-pagan-that-is-demonic-name-his-name-is-yahooshua.

106.Does 'Jesus' really mean 'Hail, Zeus'?, https://www.compellingtruth.org/Jesus-Hail-Zeus.html (last visited on November 16, 2023).

107.Kepha, Servant of YaHVaH, The Lies About Jesus Christ, http://assemblyofthekingdomofheaven.org/messages/LiesAboutJesusChrist.aspx (last visited on November 16, 2023).

108.Kepha, Servant of YaHVaH, The Lies About Jesus Christ, http://assemblyofthekingdomofheaven.org/messages/LiesAboutJesusChrist.aspx (last visited on November 16,

2023).

109.YAHSHUA – The True Name Of Our Savior And It's Importance For Use, http://yahweh.com/the-name-of-yahshua.html (last visited on November 16, 2023).

110.YAHSHUA – The True Name Of Our Savior And It's Importance For Use, http://yahweh.com/the-name-of-yahshua.html (last visited on November 16, 2023).

111.YAHSHUA – The True Name Of Our Savior And It's Importance For Use, http://yahweh.com/the-name-of-yahshua.html (last visited on November 16, 2023).

112.YAHSHUA – The True Name Of Our Savior And It's Importance For Use, http://yahweh.com/the-name-of-yahshua.html (last visited on November 16, 2023).

113.Altar of Zeus at Pergamon, Turkey: the Throne of Satan, https://voyageturkey.net/temple-altar-of-zeus-in-perga mon/ (last visited on November 16, 2023).

114.Michael Brown, What is the Original Hebrew Name for Jesus? And is it True that the Name Jesus is Really a Pagan Corruption of the Name Zeus?, January 3, 2013, https://askdrbrown.org/article/what-is-the-original-hebr ew-name-for-jesus.

115.Michael Brown, What is the Original Hebrew Name for Jesus? And is it True that the Name Jesus is Really a Pagan Corruption of the Name Zeus?, January

3, 2013,
https://askdrbrown.org/article/what-is-the-original-hebr
ew-name-for-jesus.

116.Michael Brown, What is the Original Hebrew
Name for Jesus? And is it True that the Name Jesus is
Really a Pagan Corruption of the Name Zeus?, January
3, 2013,
https://askdrbrown.org/article/what-is-the-original-hebr
ew-name-for-jesus.

117.Tuvia Pollack, Why do Israelis call Jesus
"Yeshu"?, Kehila News, November 23, 2021,
https://news.kehila.org/why-do-israelis-call-jesus-yesh
u/. Jesus vs. Yeshua?, One For Israel,
https://www.oneforisrael.org/bible-based-teaching-fro
m-israel/jesus-vs-yeshua/.

118.Tuvia Pollack, Why do Israelis call Jesus
"Yeshu"?, Kehila News, November 23, 2021,
https://news.kehila.org/why-do-israelis-call-jesus-yesh
u/.

119.Babylonian Talmud: Tractate Sanhedrin, Folio
43a, wherein the name "Yeshu" is used as the name for
Jesus,
http://www.come-and-hear.com/sanhedrin/sanhedrin_4
3.html#43a_34 (last visited on November 15, 2023).
Compare to Talmud: Tractate Sanhedrin, Folio 43a, on
the Sarian website wherein the name "Jesus" is used to
refer to Christ,
https://www.sefaria.org/Sanhedrin.43a.20?lang=bi (last
visited on November 11, 2023).

120.The Jewish Life of Christ, Being the Sepher
Toldoth Jeshu or Book of the Generation of Jesus,
Translated From the Hebrew, Edited by G.W. Foote &

J.M. Wheeler,
http://www.ftarchives.net/foote/toldoth/tjtitle.htm (last
visited on November 15, 2023).

121.Nesta Webster, Secret Societies and Subversive
Movements,
https://www.gutenberg.org/files/19104/19104-h/19104
-h.htm#fna82 (last visited on November 16, 2023). The
Jewish Life of Christ, Being the Sepher Toldoth Jeshu
or Book of the Generation of Jesus, Translated From
the Hebrew, Edited by G.W. Foote & J.M. Wheeler,
http://www.ftarchives.net/foote/toldoth/tjtitle.htm (last
visited on November 15, 2023).

122.Michael L. Rodkinson: The History of the Talmud;
http://www.come-and-hear.com/talmud/rodkin_ii3.htm
l#E27 (web address current as of February 8, 2004).

123.Michael Hoffman & Alan R. Critchley, The Truth
About the Talmud,
http://www.hoffman-info.com/talmudtruth.html
(current as of September 12, 2001).

124.Michael Hoffman & Alan R. Critchley, The Truth
About the Talmud,
http://www.hoffman-info.com/talmudtruth.html
(current as of September 12, 2001).

125.Michael Hoffman & Alan R. Critchley, The Truth
About the Talmud,
http://www.hoffman-info.com/talmudtruth.html
(current as of September 12, 2001).

126.Michael Hoffman, *Judaism Discovered*, at 534
(2008).

127.Michael Hoffman, *Judaism Discovered*, at 196 (2008).

128.Babylonian Talmud: *Tractate Sanhedrin, Folio 90a*, Sanhedrin Translated into English with Notes, Glossary and Indices Chapters I - VI by Jacob Shachter, Chapters VII - XI
by H. Freedman, B.A., Ph.D., Under the Editorship of Rabbi Dr I. Epstein B.A., Ph.D., D. Lit. (1961), *available at*
http://www.come-and-hear.com/sanhedrin/sanhedrin_9 0.html.

129.Michael Hoffman, *Judaism Discovered*, at 534 (2008).

130.Tim Kelley, Ami Yisrael, Circumcision According to Paul, January 29, 2019,
https://www.amiyisrael.org/articles/CircumcisionAccor dingToPaul/CircumcisionAccordingtoPaul.html.

131.About Us, 119 Ministries,
https://www.119ministries.com/about-us/ (last visited on November 17, 2023).

132.Circumcision, The Eternal Sign, Part 2, 119 Ministries,
https://www.119ministries.com/teachings/video-teachi ngs/detail/circumcision-the-eternal-sign-part-2/. But see Paul Parsons, Brit Milah, Should a Christian Be Cricumcised?,
https://www.hebrew4christians.com/Articles/Circumci sion/circumcision.html (last visited on November 17, 2023).

133.Tree of Life Bible Society,
https://tlvbiblesociety.org/ (last visited on February 1,

2024).

134. Tongue, American Dictionary of the English Language, https://webstersdictionary1828.com/Dictionary/tongue (last visited on January 26, 2024).

135. Tongue, American Dictionary of the English Language, https://webstersdictionary1828.com/Dictionary/tongue (last visited on January 26, 2024).

136. Hebrew Wod of the Day, Yosef, Joseph, Jerusalem Prayer Team, https://hebrew.jerusalemprayerteam.org/joseph/ (last visited on February 3, 2024). See also Julien Miquel, Yosef: How to Pronounce Joseph?, February 27, 2021, https://www.youtube.com/watch?v=wfYlm-DyIKE.

137. Jacob, Behind the Name, https://www.behindthename.com/name/jacob (last visited on February 3, 2024). See also Yaakov: How to Pronounce Jacob in Hebrew?, February 27, 2021, https://www.youtube.com/watch?v=XViI1d-JINs.

138. Jesus vs. Yeshua: Are They Really the Same Messiah??, Lapid Judaism, November 10, 2022, https://www.youtube.com/watch?v=Dt5WzZXhomw.

139. Lapid, Our Mission & Vision, https://www.lapidjudaism.org/about-lapid-judasim/mission-vision (last visited on January 20, 2024).

140. Is Lapid Judaism "Orthodox?", https://www.lapidjudaism.org/about-lapid-judasim (last visited on January 20, 2024).

141. Yeshua Centered Judasim,
https://www.lapidjudaism.org/about-lapid-judasim
(last visited on January 20, 2024).

142. Yeshua the Pharisee! This Changes Everything,
Lapid Judaism, August 25, 2022,
https://www.youtube.com/watch?v=nBFl-TWqFzA&t
=981s.

143. March 18, 2024, email from Edward Hendrie to
_____ _____.

144. March 18, 2024, email from _____ _____ to
Edward Hendrie.

145. March 18, 2024, email from Edward Hendrie to
_____ _____.

146. The Fig Tree Generation,
https://thefigtreegeneration.net/ (last visited on July 22,
2024).

147. R.B. YERBY, THE ONCE AND FUTURE
ISRAEL, p. 73-75 (1977).

148. See R.B. YERBY, THE ONCE AND FUTURE
ISRAEL, p. 47 (1977).

# Other books available from Great Mountain Publishing®

**Hoax of Biblical Proportions**
*Edward Hendrie*
ISBN: 978-1-943056-18-7

Satan knows that God has promised to preserve his words found in the Holy Scriptures, so it would be futile for him to try to destroy them. Thus, Satan's strategy is to obscure God's words by flooding the world with counterfeit Bibles. That way, he can flimflam people into reading his corrupt Bibles instead of God's infallible Scriptures. The devil can then lead men astray from the true gospel. This book will prove that the Authorized (King James) Version of the Holy Bible is given by inspiration of God. It will reveal how Satan is using profane Bible versions to divert the world away from God's inspired Holy Scriptures. The changes in the new Bible versions are not merely cosmetic for ease of reading, as claimed by the publishers; they change doctrine. The new Bible versions confuse churches and demoralize the world by proclaiming a different Jesus and a different gospel from what is in God's inspired King James Holy Bible.

## Vaccine Danger: Quackery and Sin
*Edward Hendrie*
ISBN: 978-1-943056-17-0

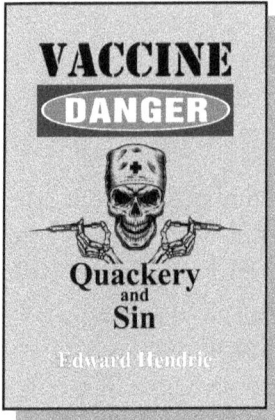

This book reveals the most significant medical fraud in history. The theory that you can prevent illness by injecting poisons into the bodies of healthy people is dangerous quackery and sin. All true science has proven the practice of vaccination to be ineffective and unsafe. But the medical establishment has been lured into the superstitious practice, hook, line, and sinker. It is not merely a matter of ignorance that the debilitating practice flourishes. It is, at its core, being promoted by those who know it is unsafe and ineffective. There is a malevolent spirit behind the practice. It is part of a conspiracy against God and man. While most doctors are unwitting, some are willing minions of that old serpent, called the Devil, and Satan, who are quite happy to kill people for profit. Jesus describes such men: "Ye are of your father the devil, and the lusts of your father ye will do. He was a murderer from the beginning, and abode not in the truth, because there is no truth in him. When he speaketh a lie, he speaketh of his own: for he is a liar, and the father of it." John 8:44.

# The Sphere of Influence: The Heliocentric Perversion of the Gospel

*Edward Hendrie*

ISBN: 978-1-943056-06-4

This book is a sequel to *The Greatest Lie on Earth (Expanded Edition): Proof That Our World Is Not a Moving Globe.* It will primarily focus on the infiltration into the church of the superstitious myth of heliocentrism and how that infiltration has served to undermine the gospel. The gospel is the entire Holy Bible, not just some of it. Matthew 4:4. Christian belief is an all or nothing proposition. "All scripture is given by inspiration of God, and is profitable for doctrine, for reproof, for correction, for instruction in righteousness." 2 Timothy 3:16. God's account of his creation is part and parcel of the gospel. A person with genuine faith believes what Jesus said about both heavenly and earthly things. "If I have told you earthly things, and ye believe not, how shall ye believe, if I tell you of heavenly things?" John 3:12. Jesus is God. Jesus created all things in heaven and on earth. See Colossians 1:16-18. God has revealed himself through his creation. "[T]hat which may be known of God is manifest in them; for God hath shewed it unto them. For the invisible things of him from the creation of the world are clearly seen, being understood by the things that are made, even his eternal power and Godhead; so that they are without excuse." Romans 1:19-20. If men have a misunderstanding of God's creation, they will also have a misunderstanding of who God is. If people believe in a creation that does not exist, they consequently also believe in a creator that does not exist. It is essential, therefore, to have an accurate understanding of God's creation. God did not make a movable, spherical earth. If men believe in a heliocentric creation, they will necessarily believe in a heliocentric creator. A heliocentric creation does not exist. So also, a heliocentric creator does not exist. A heliocentric creator is a false god. We have been warned to avoid the preaching of a false gospel, which presents a false Jesus. "For if he that cometh preacheth another Jesus, whom we have not preached, or if ye receive another spirit, which ye have not received, or another gospel, which ye have not accepted, ye might well bear with him." 2 Corinthians 11:4.

**The Greatest Lie on Earth**
**Proof That Our World Is Not a Moving Globe**
*Edward Hendrie*
ISBN-13: 978-1-943056-01-9

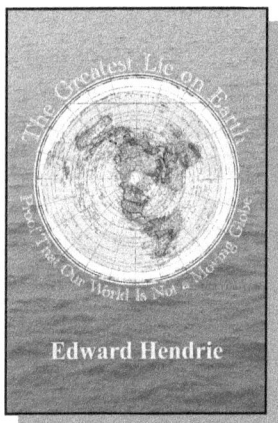

This book reveals the mother of all conspiracies. It sets forth biblical proof and irrefutable evidence that will cause the scales to fall from your eyes and reveal that the world you thought existed is a myth. The most universally accepted scientific belief today is that the earth is a globe, spinning on its axis at a speed of approximately 1,000 miles per hour at the equator, while at the same time it is orbiting the sun at approximately 66,600 miles per hour. All of this is happening as the sun, in turn, is supposed to be hurtling through the Milky Way galaxy at approximately 500,000 miles per hour. The Milky Way galaxy, itself, is alleged to be racing through space at a speed ranging from 300,000 to 1,340,000 miles per hour. What most people are not told is that the purported spinning, orbiting, and speeding through space has never been proven. In fact, every scientific experiment that has ever been performed to determine the motion of the earth has proven that the earth is stationary. Yet, textbooks ignore the scientific proof that contradicts the myth of a spinning and orbiting globe. Christian schools have been hoodwinked into teaching heliocentrism, despite the clear teaching in the Bible that the earth is not a sphere and does not move. This book reveals the evil forces behind the heliocentric deception, and why scientists and the Christian churches have gone along with it.

**The Greatest Lie on Earth (Expanded Edition)**
**Proof That Our World Is Not a Moving Globe**
*Edward Hendrie*
ISBN-13: 978-1943056-03-3

This book is an expanded edition of *The Greatest Lie on Earth*. It contains more than 1,000 pages of authoritative evidence with more than 1,300 endnotes that document proof beyond any doubt that the earth is flat and stationary. The book reveals the mother of all conspiracies. It sets forth biblical proof and irrefutable evidence that will cause the scales to fall from your eyes and reveal that the world you thought existed is a myth. The most universally accepted scientific belief today is that the earth is a globe, spinning on its axis at a speed of approximately 1,000 miles per hour at the equator, while at the same time it is orbiting the sun at approximately 66,600 miles per hour. All of this is happening as the sun, in turn, is supposed to be hurtling through the Milky Way galaxy at approximately 500,000 miles per hour. The Milky Way galaxy, itself, is alleged to be racing through space at a speed ranging from 300,000 to 1,340,000 miles per hour. What most people are not told is that the purported spinning, orbiting, and speeding through space has never been proven. In fact, every scientific experiment that has ever been performed to determine the motion of the earth has proven that the earth is stationary. Yet, textbooks ignore the scientific proof that contradicts the myth of a spinning and orbiting globe. Christian schools have been hoodwinked into teaching heliocentrism, despite the clear teaching in the Bible that the earth is not a sphere and does not move. This book reveals the evil forces behind the heliocentric deception, and why scientists and the Christian churches have gone along with it.

**Antichrist: The Beast Revealed**
*Edward Hendrie*
ISBN-13: 978-0-9832627-8-7

The antichrist is among us, here and now. This book proves it by comparing the biblical prophecies about the antichrist with the evidence that those prophecies have been fulfilled. This book documents the man of sin's esoteric confession that he is the antichrist. You will learn how the antichrist has changed times and laws as prophesied by Daniel, and how he is today sitting in the temple of God, "shewing himself that he is God," in fulfillment of Paul's prophecy in 2 Thessalonians 2:4. The beast of Revelation has come into the world, "after the working of Satan with all power and signs and lying wonders, and with all deceivableness of unrighteousness," as prophesied in 2 Thessalonians 2:10. The antichrist's adeptness as a hypocrite is the reason for his evil success. Indeed, to be the antichrist, his evil character must be concealed beneath a facade of piety. "And no marvel; for Satan himself is transformed into an angel of light. Therefore it is no great thing if his ministers also be transformed as the ministers of righteousness; whose end shall be according to their works." 2 Corinthians 11:14-15. The key to revealing the identity of the antichrist is to uncover his hypocrisy. Because the hypocrisy of the antichrist is so extreme, those who have been hoodwinked by his religious doctrines will be shocked to learn of it. This book exposes the concealed iniquity of the antichrist and juxtaposes it against his publicly proclaimed false persona of righteousness, thus bringing into clear relief that man of sin, the son of perdition, who is truly a ravening wolf in sheep's clothing, speaking lies in hypocrisy. See Matthew 7:15 and 1 Timothy 4:1-3.

**9/11-Enemies Foreign and Domestic**
*Edward Hendrie*
ISBN-13: 978-0983262732

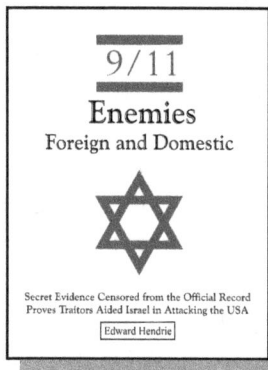

9/11-Enemies Foreign and Domestic proves beyond a reasonable doubt that the U.S. Government's conspiracy theory of the attacks on September 11, 2001, is a preposterous cover story. The evidence in 9/11-Enemies Foreign and Domestic has been suppressed from the official government reports and censored from the mass media. The evidence proves that powerful Zionists ordered the 9/11 attacks, which were perpetrated by Israel's Mossad, aided and abetted by treacherous high officials in the U.S. Government. 9/11-Enemies Foreign and Domestic identifies the traitors by name and details their subversive crimes. There is sufficient evidence in 9/11-Enemies Foreign and Domestic to indict important officials of the U.S. Government for high treason. The reader will understand how the U.S. Government really works and what Sir John Harrington (1561-1612) meant when he said: "Treason doth never prosper: what's the reason? Why if it prosper, none dare call it treason." There are millions of Americans who have taken an oath to defend the U.S. Constitution against all enemies foreign and domestic. The mass media, which is under the control of a disloyal cabal, keeps those patriotic Americans ignorant of the traitors among them. J. Edgar Hoover, former Director of the FBI, explained: "The individual is handicapped by coming face-to-face with a conspiracy so monstrous-he simply cannot believe it exists." 9/11-Enemies Foreign and Domestic erases any doubt about the existence of the monstrous conspiracy described by Hoover and arms the reader with the knowledge required to save our great nation. "My people are destroyed for lack of knowledge." Hosea 4:6.

**Solving the Mystery of BABYLON THE GREAT**
*Edward Hendrie*
ISBN-13: 978-0983262701

"Attorney and Christian researcher Edward Hendrie investigates and reveals one of the greatest exposés of all time. . . . a book you don't want to miss. Solving the Mystery of Babylon the Great is packed with documentation. Never before have the crypto-Jews who seized the reins of power in Rome been put under such intense scrutiny." Texe Marrs, Power of Prophecy. The evidence presented in this book leads to the ineluctable conclusion that the Roman Catholic Church was established by crypto-Jews as a false "Christian" front for a Judaic/Babylonian religion. That religion is the core of a world conspiracy against man and God. That is not a conspiracy theory based upon speculation, but rather the hard truth based upon authoritative evidence, which is documented in this book. Texe Marrs explains in his foreword to the book: "Who is Mystery Babylon? What is the meaning of the sinister symbols found in these passages? Which city is being described as the 'great city' so full of sin and decadence, and who are its citizens? Why do the woman and beast of Revelation seek the destruction of the holy people, the saints and martyrs of Jesus? What does it all mean for you and me today? Solving the Mystery of Babylon the Great answers these questions and more. Edward Hendrie's discoveries are not based on prejudice but on solid evidence aligned forthrightly with the 'whole counsel of God.' He does not condone nor will he be a part of any project in which Bible verses are taken out of context, or in which scriptures are twisted to mean what they do not say. Again and again you will find that Mr. Hendrie documents his assertions, backing up what he says with historical facts and proofs. Most important is that he buttresses his findings with scriptural understanding. The foundation for his research is sturdy because it is based on the bedrock of God's unshakeable Word."

**The Anti-Gospel**
*Edward Hendrie*
ISBN-13: 978-0983262749

The
Anti-Gospel

The Perversion of
Christ's Grace Gospel

Edward Hendrie uses God's word to strip the sheep's clothing from false Christian ministers and expose them as ravening wolves preaching an anti-gospel. The anti-gospel is based on a myth that all men have a will that is free from the bondage of sin to choose whether to believe in Jesus. The Holy Bible, however, states that all men are spiritually dead and cannot believe in Jesus unless they are born again of the Holy Spirit. Ephesians 2:1-7; John 3:3-8. God has chosen his elect to be saved by his grace through faith in Jesus Christ. Ephesians 1:3-9; 2:8-10. God imbues his elect with the faith needed to believe in Jesus. Hebrews 12:2; John 1:12-13. The devil's false gospel contradicts the word of God and reverses the order of things. Under the anti-gospel, instead of a sovereign God choosing his elect, sovereign man decides whether to choose God. The calling of the Lord Jesus Christ is effectual; all who are chosen for salvation will believe in Jesus. John 6:37-44. The anti-gospel has a false Jesus, who only offers the possibility of salvation, with no assurance. The anti-gospel blasphemously makes God out to be a liar by denying the total depravity of man and the sovereign election of God. All who preach that false gospel are under a curse from God. Galatians 1:6-9.

**Bloody Zion**
*Edward Hendrie*
ISBN-13: 978-0983262763

Jesus told Pontius Pilate: "My kingdom is not of this world." John 18:36. God has a spiritual Zion that is in a heavenly Jerusalem. Hebrews 12:22; Revelation 21:10. Jesus Christ is the chief corner stone laid by God in Zion. 1 Peter 2:6. Those who believe in Jesus Christ are living stones in the spiritual house of God. 1 Peter 2:5; Ephesians 2:20-22. Believers are in Jesus and Jesus is in believers. John 14:20; 17:20-23. All who are elected by God to believe in Jesus Christ are part of the heavenly Zion, without regard to whether they are Jews or Gentiles. Romans 10:12. Satan is a great adversary of God, who has created his own mystery religions. During the Babylonian captivity (2 Chronicles 36:20), an occult society of Jews replaced God's commands with Satan's Babylonian dogma. Their new religion became Judaism. Jesus explained the corruption of the Judaic religion: "Howbeit in vain do they worship me, teaching for doctrines the commandments of men." Mark 7:7. Jesus revealed the Satanic origin of Judaism when he stated: "Ye are of your father the devil, and the lusts of your father ye will do." John 8:44. Babylonian Judaism remains the religion of the Jews today. Satan has infected many nominal "Christian" denominations with his Babylonian occultism, which has given rise to "Christian" Zionism.

"Christian" Zionism advocates a counterfeit, earthly Zion, within which fleshly Jews take primacy over the spiritual church of Jesus Christ. This book exposes "Christian" Zionism as a false gospel and subversive political movement that sustains Israel's war against God and man.

**Murder, Rape, and Torture in a Catholic Nunnery**
*Edward Hendrie*
ISBN-13: 978-1-943056-00-2

There has probably not been a person more maligned by the powerful forces of the Roman Catholic Church than Maria Monk. In 1836 she published the famous book, *Awful Disclosures of the Hotel Dieu Nunnery of Montreal.* In that book, she told of murder, rape, and torture behind the walls of the cloistered nunnery. Because the evidence was verifiably true, the Catholic hierarchy found it necessary to fabricate evidence and suborn perjury in an attempt to destroy the credibility of Maria Monk. The Catholic Church has kept up the character assassination of Maria Monk now for over 175 years. Even today, there can be found on the internet websites devoted to libeling Maria Monk. Edward Hendrie has examined the evidence and set it forth for the readers to decide for themselves whether Maria Monk was an impostor, as claimed by the Roman Catholic Church, or whether she was a brave victim. An objective view of the evidence leads to the ineluctable conclusion that Maria Monk told the truth about what happened behind the walls of the Hotel Dieu Nunnery of Montreal. The Roman Catholic Church, which is the most powerful religious and political organization in the world, has engaged in an unceasing campaign of vilification against Maria Monk. Their crusade against Maria Monk, however, can only affect the opinion of the uninformed. It cannot change the evidence. The evidence speaks clearly to those who will look at the case objectively. The evidence reveals that the much maligned Maria Monk was a reliable witness who made awful but accurate disclosures about life in a cloistered nunnery.

## What Shall I Do to Inherit Eternal Life?
*Edward Hendrie*
ISBN-13: 978-0983262770

A certain ruler posed to Jesus the most important question ever asked: "Good Master, what shall I do to inherit eternal life?" (Luke 18:18) The man came to the right person. Jesus is God, and therefore his answer to that question is authoritative. This book examines Jesus' surprising answer and definitively explains how one inherits eternal life. This is a book about God's revelation to man. Except for the Holy Bible, this is the most important book you will ever read.

**The Damnable Heresy Of Salvation by Dead Faith (Expanded Edition)**
*Edward Hendrie*
ISBN 13: 978-1943056118

Good works follow salvation; they do not earn salvation. Good works do not save us. The works of faith are those works ordained and performed by God through the believer. They are the result of faith. It is that perfect faith that justifies the believer. "For by grace are ye saved through faith; and that not of yourselves: it is the gift of God: Not of works, lest any man should boast. For we are his workmanship, created in Christ Jesus unto good works, which God hath before ordained that we should walk in them. For we are his workmanship, created in Christ Jesus unto good works, which God hath before ordained that we should walk in them." Ephesians 2:8-10. In Romans, chapters 6 and 8, Paul explains faith without good works cannot save. Paul says that God's elect "walk not after the flesh, but after the Spirit." Romans 8:1. He states that those who do not walk in the Spirit but instead walk in the flesh "shall not inherit the kingdom of God." Galatians 5:15-25. John explains: "If we say that we have fellowship with him, and walk in darkness, we lie, and do not the truth: But if we walk in the light, as he is in the light, we have fellowship one with another, and the blood of Jesus Christ his Son cleanseth us from all sin." 1 John 1:6-7. James asks a rhetorical question: "What doth it profit, my brethren, though a man say he hath faith, and have not works? can faith save him?" James 2:14. James succinctly explains that "faith without works is dead." James 2:20. The pronouncement in James that true faith bears the fruit of good works is a theme found in the gospel. But some perniciously preach that God saves a person by faith that has no good works.

That is one of the "damnable heresies" about which Peter warned. See 2 Peter 2:1-22.

**Rome's Responsibility for the Assassination of Abraham Lincoln, With an Appendix Containing Conversations Between Abraham Lincoln and Charles Chiniquy**
*Thomas M. Harris*
ISBN-13: 978-0983262794

The author of this book, General Thomas Maley Harris, was a medical doctor, who recruited and served as commander of the Tenth West Virginia Volunteers during the Civil War. He rose in rank through meritorious service to become a brigadier general in the Union Army. General Harris established a reputation for faithfulness, industriousness, intelligence, and efficiency. He was noted for his leadership in preparing his troops and leading them in battle. He was brevetted a major general for "gallant conduct in the assault on Petersburg." After the Civil War, General Harris served one term as a representative in the West Virginia legislature, and was West Virginia's Adjutant General from 1869 to 1870. General Harris was a member of the Military Commission that tried and convicted the conspirators who assassinated President Abraham Lincoln. He had first hand knowledge of the sworn testimony of the witnesses in that trial. This book summarizes the salient evidence brought out during the military trial and adds information from other sources to present before the public the ineluctable conclusion that the assassination of Abraham Lincoln was the work of the Roman Catholic Church. The Roman Catholic Church has been largely successful in suppressing the circulation of this book. This book has never been given a place on bookstore shelves, as it exposed too much for the Roman Catholic hierarchy to tolerate. Any display of this book would bring an instant boycott of the bookstore. It is only now, in the age of the internet, where the marketplace of ideas has been opened wide, that this book can be found by those searching for the truth of who was behind the assassination of Abraham Lincoln.

The above books can be ordered from bookstores and from internet sites, including, but not limited to:

https://greatmountainpublishing.com
www.antichristconspiracy.com
www.911enemies.com
www.mysterybabylonthegreat.net
www.antigospel.com
https://play.google.com
www.barnesandnoble.com
www.amazon.com

Edward Hendrie
edwardhendrie@gmail.com

www.ingramcontent.com/pod-product-compliance
Lightning Source LLC
Chambersburg PA
CBHW071221090426
42736CB00014B/2923